I WILL NOT LEAVE YOU
 COMFORTLESS

Also by Jeremy Jackson

In Summer

Life at These Speeds

I WILL NOT LEAVE YOU COMFORTLESS

A MEMOIR

JEREMY JACKSON

milkweed
editions

© 2012, Text by Jeremy Jackson
All rights reserved. Except for brief quotations in critical articles or reviews, no part of this book may be reproduced in any manner without prior written permission from the publisher: Milkweed Editions, 1011 Washington Avenue South, Suite 300, Minneapolis, Minnesota 55415.
(800) 520-6455
www.milkweed.org

Published 2013 by Milkweed Editions
Printed in the United States
Cover design by Christian Fuenfhausen
Cover photos © Shutterstock
Author photo © Victoria Palermo
Interior design by Connie Kuhnz
The text of this book is set in Arno Pro.
13 14 15 16 17   5 4 3 2 1
First Paperback Printing
ISBN: 978-1-57131-343-0

Please turn to the back of this book for a list of the sustaining funders of Milkweed Editions.

The Library of Congress has catalogued the hardcover edition as follows:

Jackson, Jeremy, 1973–
    I will not leave you comfortless : a memoir / Jeremy Jackson. — 1st ed.
        p.   cm.
    ISBN 978-1-57131-332-4 (acid-free paper)
    1. Jackson, Jeremy, 1973–   2. Authors, American—21st century—Biography.
I. Title.
    PS3610.A352Z46 2012
    813'.6—dc23
    [B]
                                                                          2012007803

This book is printed on acid-free paper.

Contents

I WILL NOT LEAVE YOU
COMFORTLESS

the first part

A Storm

On the last Wednesday of April, 1983, my grandmother went to a funeral. She drove from the farm to Windsor through the early afternoon sunlight, past pastures where the grass was shin high and rising, past full creeks, past newly plowed fields. In town, the last tulips bloomed in front yards and side yards, the sidewalks were swept, and the streets were shaded by leaves that as of a week ago hadn't even been born. This was spring in Missouri.

She had heard on the radio about the thunderstorms, but there was no sign of them yet. The day was quiet. She walked from the parking lot to the church through a breeze with no hint of threat to it. She was not a nervous woman, nor unfamiliar with the storms of her part of the country. She had lived in western Missouri her whole life, and she didn't consider changing the course of her day just because storms were near.

That said, when the funeral was over and she had played the last sustained chord on the organ, she headed straight home. Within the course of an hour, the sky had changed. The sun had slipped behind a veil of high clouds so that the day was still bright, but there were no shadows anymore. She drove west, and once she left the trees and houses of town she could see the storm clouds in front of her. They were close.

Really, it was a race. She was on a collision course with the storms, and it was simply a matter of who would reach the farm first. The clouds that were approaching were not pleasant clouds. They were black and moving fast, like the flagships of night.

She left the blacktop and headed up the gravel road. Back toward town, there was still blue sky visible. Just a little badge of it in her rearview mirror.

She had a couple of miles to go on the white, straight-shot road. Dust billowed behind her. The rumble of the tires cruising over the gravel masked any sound of thunder.

She was almost home.

At last she pulled into the driveway of the farmhouse, gathered her purse and sheet music, and got out of the car. The clouds were nearly overhead. The air was moist and stuffy, like a greenhouse. She went inside. She set her purse on the kitchen counter as a rapidly expanding whooshing sound came from all directions at once, and the house's joints began to creak inside the walls. She looked out the kitchen window and saw the wind sweeping the yard in one sustained and still-gathering blast.

Then rain hit the panes.

She watched the storm. She moved through the strange, dusky light of the farmhouse, looking out the bedroom window, then the front door, then the side door. She thought about Grandpa, who had taken some calves to the sale barn and was now out in the storm. She thought about dinner. She thought about the funeral she'd just been to. It was one of nearly thirty she played for that year, and she hadn't known the man well. She thought about the garden and hoped the rain wasn't too much for it. But before long, the rain was letting up.

At 3:15, she sat down and wrote a letter to my family, as she did nearly every week.

It's really dark, she started, *looks like about 6:30 and it's the middle of the afternoon—We've had a big rain this afternoon.*

She heard an engine and looked through the dining room window to see Grandpa's headlights.

Daddy took the rest of the calves to the sale this afternoon and he is just now getting home.

Sixty miles east, at that moment, I was on my way home from school. Mom had picked up Susan and me in dinky old Russellville, and now we were driving through the countryside toward our farm, followed by a car containing two of Mom's piano students and one of their mothers.

The storm that had swept over Grandma now glowered on our horizon, and I didn't care for it. I was a ten-year-old who knew too much about storms. They showed us informational films each year at school, films from twenty years ago, when the kids wore clothes that seemed more appropriate for church, films that strived to impart to us an awareness of the fact that tornadoes would, given the chance, kill us. The storm that faced us fit the profile of a tornado spawner if I'd ever seen one: greenish, from the southwest, April, midafternoon.

The films were clear: basements are your only hope.

We didn't have a basement.

Mon. was such a beautiful day, Grandma continued. *Washed 2 loads of clothes, the back bedroom curtains and cleaned that room. About 3 o'clock we set out 3 doz. cauliflower plants, 2 doz. broccoli—2 more rows of potatoes and 2 rows of green beans. Don't think ever in my life it made me feel so bad, actually thought I was coming down with something.*

Tue.—couldn't do the curtains, was too windy—then last night was Sewing Club—this morn., washed the dining r. & front bedroom curtains and hung them out . . . I got all the curtains pressed before I left at 1 o'clock for the funeral, so have had plenty to do today, but did feel more normal this morn.

When we got home, I wrapped myself in a blanket, put on my fake plastic batting helmet, and went into the house's only interior room: the sewing closet under the stairs. I could hear the piano lessons well because the piano was right next to the sewing closet door. I stood in the tiny closet and looked at the wall of shelves filled with spools, bobbins, and jars of buttons. I could hear the thunder. Muffled, thuddy thunder. And I could hear my quickened heartbeat. There was no place to sit. This was not good at all, this basementless tornado-bait farmhouse.

After several minutes, I heard the back door of the house open and close. It meant Elizabeth, my oldest sister, had made it home. I emerged to greet her, only to find not Elizabeth but the mother who had brought the piano students. She'd been waiting in her car.

"I think that's more than just a regular storm," she said to my mother. "Do you have a basement?"

I returned to the closet. Chewed my fingernails. Worried about Elizabeth.

Daddy planted 4 rows of sweet corn this morn. It should be well packed in the ground after this rain.

We are really proud of Elizabeth winning the trip to Wash. D.C., that's just great. Now Darrell would you write another article for the paper for me about this and about the Distinguished Am. High School Student Award she has received—we will save all the track records for another time.

Daddy got good price for his calves, the best price was some at $74.75 (steers), had 5 bulls at $70.75, heifers at $63.30—he thought that was good for heifers. They are better prices than he got last year—

Must stop and get supper—

Love from both
Mother and Daddy

P.S. Daddy saved 4 calves to butcher—

Elizabeth, on the other hand, didn't worry about storms.

She left school and drove through Russellville—the curbless, peeling-paint town of seven hundred. Soon she entered the country-side. Black cattle lay in the corner of a pasture. A crow wheeled over the wind-wracked trees. For Elizabeth, the drive home was always satisfying, and the pickup—especially at speeds over sixty—had a nice floaty ride. One time, the truck had raced Tom Claypool's car. And won.

She watched the storm as she cruised along the long, open ridge of Route U. She was thankful there had been a track meet yesterday, otherwise this wouldn't be a resting day, and she would be out on some gravel road right now, miles from school, running.

I can beat this storm, she thought and pushed the accelerator. The truck went faster.

She loved a race, and she loved to win.

She turned onto Mount Hope Road—our gravel road—just a mile and a half from the farm and faced the oncoming storm. She was going to make it. She would beat the storm home.

But the clouds were coming straight at her now, so close they filled the entire western sky, and when she crested the top of the first hill, she was met with a blast of wind so strong that it stopped the truck and sprayed gravel against the windshield.

She had time to think, So this is what a tornado is like. And she had enough calm in her—enough of the athlete's instinctiveness—to consider the safest place for her to be at this moment.

She opened the truck door, stepped into the storm, and dashed for the ditch. She crouched there with her hands over her head, her back to the storm, as the wind gusted and faded and then gusted again. Raindrops stung her back. But she soon realized the worst had passed.

After the storm's blast waned, I emerged from the closet. I walked from room to room, looking out every window at the heavy rain. Piano music continued in the living room. I went to the glassed-in back porch and saw Elizabeth running up the sidewalk. I hadn't heard the truck approach because the rain was so loud. I opened the door for her, and she ducked inside.

"Phew!" she said, water dripping off her face. She looked at me. "What are you wearing?"

Our sister, Susan, appeared in the doorway leading to the kitchen. "He was scared of the storm," she said, "so he put on that blanket and plastic hat and hid under the stairs."

I was so happy Elizabeth was home, I didn't even bother to defend myself.

"I wish I'd been under the stairs," Elizabeth said. "The weirdest thing happened."

She told us her story, and we listened, rapt, and we asked her to repeat it. The best part was when she got into the ditch, waited, then just stood up and drove home. Elizabeth! Elizabeth could survive anything.

"You mean there was actual gravel in the air?" I asked.

"Yeah, not just sand but, like, big pebbles. *Bam-bam-bam-bam!* Hitting the windshield."

"Did you leave the truck running?" Susan asked.

"Yeah!" she said, and laughed. "Luckily I put it in park!"

We laughed: Elizabeth had been in some sort of mini-tornado and had left the truck engine running. But probably it would have been funny even if she'd turned it off. Mainly we were giddy that Elizabeth was safe. We were all safe. The storm had knocked down a few small branches and sent a bucket reeling across the lawn, but that was all.

After the piano students left and the rain stopped, we went outside and looked at the truck. Much of the paint on the hood had been scoured away, and the windshield had dozens of pits and dings. But it wasn't broken.

I looked up to Elizabeth as if she were a giant. She was seven years older than I was. Her letter jacket was so heavy with medals from track and basketball, it must have weighed five pounds. She had scars on her ankles from being spiked by other runners, scars on her knees from falling on cinder tracks. She had the same dishwater-blond hair I did, and a fast-trigger jump shot so rare among girl basketball players that opponents sometimes did a double take.

I could think of nothing better to be than a Jeremy version of Elizabeth: athlete, scholar, bale-chucking, manure-shoveling farm kid, pickup racer, lifeguard, horse rider. Hers were the shoes I aimed to fill.

On the day of that storm, the one both Grandma and Elizabeth raced home, my father was working in his office in the basement of the state capitol in Jefferson City. There were no windows, and the office was so deeply buried that even the loudest thunder couldn't be heard. He was at his desk when suddenly—*blink!*—the lights went out.

Food, Animals

The way it worked is that we would stop at Alvina's house about once a week, either on the way home from Jefferson City or having come from school in Russellville. If you volunteered or were conscripted into service, you opened the car door and stepped onto the white pebbles of Alvina's driveway. Unless it was winter, you left the car door open. If Alvina was near, you said hello or waved. She was nice.

You entered the shed and went through the dim first room, then stepped down one step that was never quite where you expected it to be. There on the left was the deep cooler, and you reached down and pulled out a gallon of fresh milk, which was cold and heavy. The huge glass jar was wet because the cooler was filled with water and you lifted the jar carefully and there was no easy way to hold it. No handles. If we were picking up two gallons, someone came with you. One of your parents. Or a sister. One person could carry only one jar. That was the equation.

You now stood, holding eight pounds of milk, in one of the dark places of the world. This, though, simplified your exit. All you had to do was aim for the light coming through the doorway that led outside. And once you got the milk back into the light of day, you saw it—the milk itself—for the first time. White. You climbed back into the car and put the jar on the floor, and held it upright by squeezing it between your shins and keeping one hand on the lid. The lid itself was the size of a saucer. As the driver pulled carefully back onto the blacktop, accelerating slowly, you realized the milk was moving in the jar. You were reminded that it was liquid.

From Alvina's, you drove south to Mount Hope Road, then rolled along the gravel road—down four hills, up four hills, but not in that order—and then turned into the long driveway. The driveway traced the perimeter of a grassy hill. At a bend in the driveway you looked at the gravelly shoulder where turtles could be found surprisingly frequently—say, once a year. Tortoises. This was also the corner where long ago your sisters saw a rattlesnake and walked around it by cutting through the field. So the story went.

The car climbed the little hill—slowly—and then you saw the house, the barns. On your right was a valley of pastures and fields. There were lines of trees along the fencerows. One of the ponds was down there.

When the car got closer to the farmhouse, the terrier and the small black cat would issue forth from the front porch, and that—that moment—was one of the best parts of the day. Here was your universe, your sun and your moons. You carried the milk inside—and if anything it seemed colder now than when you'd first lifted it into your arms—you hefted it onto the counter, you unscrewed the tremendous lid, and you skimmed the cream from the top. With the cream, we would make butter or occasionally whipped cream or sometimes ice cream. As for the milk, we drank it and used it for baking and sometimes gave a splash of it to the cats. We mixed it with a dollop of yogurt and put it in a jar and put the jar in an insulated box and put the box down by the refrigerator's warm exhaust and in the morning the milk would be yogurt. During the summer, we put the milk on our cereal, and during the school year when we weren't allowed cold cereal, we drizzled a little milk on our oatmeal. Just a little. It helped cool the oatmeal. "Oatmeal, meet milk. Milk, meet oatmeal." That's the kind of thing we would say.

The milk was not pasteurized. It was not homogenized. It tasted like something. Something singular. Alvina's cow wasn't a Holstein or Jersey, or any other breed of cow that you would encounter at the state fair. There was nothing written in any textbook about this kind of cow. It was a milk cow of indeterminate origin. It was a small cow. Brown.

Those huge glass jars. We never broke a single one.

We. Us. Ours. We were five in number. We were a father, a mother, a sister, another sister, and a brother. Our father wore navy pinstriped suits and drove into Jefferson City each day, where he worked with legislators and the chief clerk and the speaker of the house and his own staff of researchers. The soles of men's shoes clicked on the polished floors of the long corridors. The parking garage was a spiral. The capitol building sat on a bluff overlooking the muddy Missouri River.

Our father drove home at night and changed out of his suit and into khaki work pants and a blue shirt and then he did chores. He fed the cows and horses and cats. Closed the chicken coop. Other times he cut brush with the tractor, chainsawed, stacked hay bales in the hayloft, mended fences, helped a cow deliver her calf in the middle of the night. There was a row of boots on the back porch: rain boots, work boots, steel-toe boots, snow boots.

Our father who came from a farm not so far away, who had gone to the state university and married our mother there, then continued on to a university on the East Coast that was so famous that simply stating the fact of his enrollment there was essentially a form of bragging, and therefore the name was rarely spoken. Our father who was a doctor, but not that kind of doctor. The room in the house that we called the study—but which was also a bedroom—had three walls of bookshelves, floor to ceiling, the titles inscrutable. Greek and Latin. Plato and Augustine. He would sit in a chair after dark. Just a regular chair, not a soft one. And he would read and touch his mustache absentmindedly.

Our father had a mustache. Always had.

Food. Animals. You lay in bed and thought. Now that it was summer, your bed was pushed up against the window, and your head was by the window, and the window was open and you could hear the bullfrogs at the west pond talking and the bullfrogs at the east pond talking and from everywhere else you heard crickets. You could hear a car on the gravel road a long way away, moving, making a whooshing noise on the gravel, growing louder, cresting a hill, then fading. Who was that, out driving in the night? Maybe it was Elizabeth, who was out with her boyfriend, Wayne Elwood. Maybe not. Light bloomed up through the open stairwell and shone against one wall of your room. Dad was still awake, but it was quiet down there, down in the living room. You listened and you waited and then you heard him turn a page.

You rolled over and you looked at the dark, open doorway to your sisters' room. Then you heard something. A faint jingling. A rhythmic jingling. Outside. You rolled onto your stomach and looked out the window, but it was dark, very dark out there. But the noise, you knew what it was. It was the terrier, Teddy. His vaccination tag—the little aluminum vaccination tag—jingling against his collar as he trotted across the yard. Maybe he was about to bark at something. Maybe he sensed raccoons in the vicinity.

The jingling stopped.

"Teddy?" you called out the window.

No jingling. You knew he was standing motionless in the dark, his ears pricked up because he had heard you. He was listening.

"Teddy," you said, "go to bed."

In the other room, Susan laughed. You smiled because you had made her laugh. She was lying in her own bed, going to sleep, just like you.

You put your chin down onto the pillow, still looking out the window. You sank into the pillow up to your nose, and you could smell the pillow and the pillow blocked your nose and made breathing pleasantly difficult.

The terrier was on the move again and then the sound faded away.

From the other room, after awhile, Susan said, "Where'd he go?" She had heard him, too. She was lying by her window, too.

You said, "Around the house, I think." You wondered. You said, "Maybe he's thirsty."

You thought about that, and about the pan of water behind the cellar house where he drank. The cats drank there, too. You thought about the doghouse on the front porch, which was painted the same color as the real house. Sometimes the terrier slept in there and sometimes he didn't. It was anybody's guess. Then you thought about how if you pointed to something extremely directly—in other words, touched it—and said the terrier's name with a certain urgency, he would eat whatever you were pointing at. Or attempt to eat it. He was four years old and you'd owned him since your sixth birthday and he was a cairn terrier approximately the color of old straw. His eyes hid behind a veil of hair but he didn't seem to have any trouble seeing and sometimes for fun you would pull back his bangs and reveal his eyes and they were black.

If you were working in the garden, the terrier would join you because any kind of garden work involved edible things for him. True, if you were there, it might mean you would trick him into trying to eat a piece of wood or a grasshopper. But your mother would never trick him and if she was doing any kind of digging or weeding it meant that in all likelihood the terrier's favorite delicacy would be unearthed. Grubs. White grubs. Fat white grubs. Why did he like those so much? They were somewhat see-through.

He also liked peas. Last year when the peas were ripe you would sometimes wander into the rows of peas in the afternoon and pick a few and shell them and eat them right there and usually the terrier would be right at your heels and he would eat the hulls you dropped but also he was hoping you would give him a whole pod—peas and all—because he liked that even better than the hulls. And who wouldn't? You and Susan would give him a few whole pods, but not many. He also ate some kinds of cattle feed and occasionally poop, but that was hard to understand. Also, when the farrier came to trim the horses' hooves, he would leave the trimmed bits of hoof in the barnyard and the terrier found these to be extremely enjoyable to chew on, especially after they had dried for a few days. When they dried, they shrank and curled. He didn't eat them, he just chewed on them, but if you came too close to him when he was chewing on a horse hoof he would growl. Stay back, bucko. This is my horse hoof. So no monkey business.

He meant it. And who cared? You didn't want the horse hooves.

"Hey," you said. You had rolled onto your back and your eyes were closed.

"What?" Susan said from her bed. You could tell from her voice that she was close to sleep. Downstairs, the lights in the living room were off, but you could hear Dad in the kitchen.

"Do you remember," you said, "how Teddy ate peas last summer?" You waited awhile. "Yeah," she said.

The peas would be ready again soon. In the garden.

"Do you think he'll eat them this year?" you asked.

"Yeah . . ."

"I bet so," you said. You opened your eyes and then you closed them again and then you thought of something and you opened them.

"Hey," you said, "do you remember when Teddy ate that balloon once?"

"Yeah . . ."

You thought about it. "Me too," you said.

And it was the last thing you said, because you were falling asleep.

Mulberries were a June thing. They went from white to pink to red to black, and then they were ready. They weren't that good to eat and if you had more than a few your stomach got quarrelsome. You had to spit out the stems because they were unchewable and tasted like clover leaves. There were little bugs on the mulberries anyway. Bugs about the size of dust, but you could see them moving if you looked close. Mainly you thought about mulberries at the end of the night when you washed your feet. You went barefoot all summer and when you were running around the yard barefoot in June sometimes you weren't really thinking about what you were doing, because apparently you ran under the mulberry tree a few times and crushed a lot of fallen mulberries with your feet without even realizing it. You saw the blotches when you washed your feet at

night. You didn't mind the blotches. They were kind of like a sun-
tan; it was just something that happened in the course of the summer. You could still see the stains the next day. They didn't wash off.
You'd see them at breakfast as you sat cross-legged. They were a reminder. A reminder of themselves. You'd look at your feet and think
to yourself, oh, mulberries. They're no good to eat. You never even
realized you'd been running under the mulberry tree until later. Oh,
you'd think, mulberries.

Summertime breakfast. Certain regions of your hair were sticking up.

The day after school ended in late May, your shoes and socks
came off. But your feet were tender. Walking in the grass felt like
being tickled. If you stepped on a june bug it would buzz and you
would shriek because of how it felt. The sidewalk was rough. And
you couldn't walk on the gravel of the driveway at all because it was
just too much to take. The situation of having tender feet had no im-
mediate remedy, but you were reminded by Mom that it wouldn't
last; your feet would get tougher, and in a couple of weeks you'd be
running in the driveway, riding bikes, walking on the prickly hay in
the barn, and so forth, without even realizing you didn't have shoes
on. You would start to lose track of your shoes. Shoes? Where are my
shoes? I haven't seen my shoes in days.

You stood in the garden with Susan, clasping each other by the
shoulders, and dug your feet down into the loose soil until they disappeared and you were people without feet. You were ankle people.

The soil, for its part, was warm.

We. Us. Ours. We were five in number.

Our mother. She would cut our hair in the kitchen. We would sit
with an old sheet pinned around our necks and she would snip away.

"How old were you when you married Dad?" we would prompt.

"I was nineteen. A teenage bride," she'd tell us again. We'd laugh.
"We were so poor we ate a lot of pancakes for dinner."

Pancakes for dinner did not sound like deprivation.

Our mother. Whereas our father came from the plains of western Missouri, from tall people who worked the soil and didn't have much to say about that, our mother came from the Ozarks of southern Missouri, from people who hunted the woods and hollows and had stories that led to more stories that led to even more stories. The time the schoolteacher was sprayed by a skunk. The time the buggy tipped over. The time the roof caught on fire. The rattlesnake story, the snowstorm story, the first radio story. These stories trickled from our grandmother's generation to our mother and then to us.

Our mother who was a social worker who helped children, but whose other job was us. She did magical things: feeding us, growing food for us, sewing for us, baking bread for us, taking us to dance lessons and piano lessons and softball games. We'd walk in the door after coming home from school and smell gingerbread.

Our mother who stood by her husband in all his years of graduate school, in a time when the wives of the students joked that while their husbands got PhDs, the wives got PHTs, which stood for "Putting Hubby Through." She'd been a faculty wife. She'd had a baby in Connecticut, a baby in North Carolina, a baby in Ohio. Tenure was an elusive thing, so our mother and father decided to return to Missouri to raise their family.

There were the horses. There were the cows. There were the ducks and there were the chickens. The baby chicks hatched in June. You would wait and wait and all the hens were sitting on their eggs, and you knew exactly how many eggs they each had and you knew when they were supposed to hatch, and usually when they were supposed to hatch, they did. You could hear them in there—inside the egg!—peeping, just before they hatched. You would wait for all the eggs to hatch, and most of the time one or two eggs per batch didn't hatch and the mother hen would leave the nest with her new family, and we would take the abandoned eggs inside, and Mom would wrap them in a little towel and put them in a metal bowl on top of the stove's pilot light and sometimes—just sometimes—one of these eggs would hatch. Then you had probably saved its life. You and Susan and Mom. Plus the pilot light.

After breakfast, the first thing you did was go gather the eggs. Not the eggs with babies in them, but the new eggs. Eggs for eating. You carried a wicker basket and you went through the gate, brushing past the honeysuckle, and walked down the path to the chicken house. You let the chickens out—they were bunched at the door, waiting—and they fanned out across the yard and the mother hens were followed by the associations of puffs that were their babies. You went inside the chicken house and reached into the nesting boxes to get the new eggs. They were often warm from having been sat on. Sometimes you had to shoo an old hen off her nest so you could have her eggs. And sometimes you reached into a nest that was too high for you to see into and you felt an egg that was big and smooth and it wasn't really an egg at all and you jumped backward because what you'd just touched was a snake, which was having a nap after a snack of eggs.

To get to the blackberry patch, at the back of the farm, sometimes we drove the pickup out there. Driving in the fields was a holiday of its own. The grass would brush the underside of the pickup. Or, if we didn't drive, we walked out there. Talk about tall grass. To walk out there, you had to go through the big pasture by the north pond. That pasture had tall fescue grass you had to wade through. If you sat down, the horizon vanished, the trees on the edge of the field vanished. You could see just a few feet into the grass and you could see sky. That was all. You could flatten down the grass to make a little sitting area. You could make a path to another sitting area and have two sitting areas and a path. Of course, once the grass was cut for hay, there'd be no more of that kind of thing.

They were wild blackberries. Picking them was fun for about the first twelve berries, then it was work, but you were allowed to eat as many as you wanted. Fresh blackberries meant you got a cobbler for dinner. You could also put them on your cereal with honey. The second day, maybe we would crumble hot biscuits in bowls, then sprinkle them with berries, then add milk or cream, then add honey. It was almost the best thing a person could eat. There was no name for it, so when you wanted it you had to say the whole thing: "Biscuits with berries on them and then milk and honey in a bowl." It was a breakfast or a dessert for lunch or dinner or a snack for night. That's what it was. It was all of that.

Many of the blackberries were frozen in the freezer on the back porch. That way, in the middle of winter you might suddenly find a blackberry cobbler cooling on the counter and you would go instantly wiggly because of how lucky you were. The berries had traveled all the way from summer just to be something warm for you to eat on a cold, dark night. And who knew: you might have picked that berry right there. That exact berry . . .

The brambles would scratch you when you were picking berries. Like how a kitten scratches your arms, even though it doesn't mean to. Also, there were ticks, chiggers, and poison ivy. The hazards of the blackberry patch. You never saw any snakes out there, but for some reason you were always told that there might be snakes. A watchful eye was required.

It felt like a long way from the house, even though you could look across the pastures and see the house on the hill, residing in the elm shade. Still, it felt like you were really out somewhere. You knew the creek was not too far away. You couldn't hear any roads from there. If you looked up, maybe there was a jet making a line in the sky. Not that you could see the actual jet, just the line.

Black-eyed Susans. Daisies. Queen Anne's lace.

Summer sun. Summer heat.

Berries and more berries.

July 5: five cups. July 7: eight cups. July 9: a gallon. On the 12th: seven quarts. On the 15th: seven gallons. July 18: another five and a half gallons. The last berries were on the 21st: three and a quarter gallons.

Fresh blackberries, frozen blackberries, home-canned blackberries. Jam, jelly, juice.

Before blackberry month, there were trips to pick strawberries

at strawberry farms. For about three days you ate as many strawberries as humanly possible. The rest had to be cleaned, sliced, sug-
ared, and frozen. Then there were trips to go pick blueberries. And
then you ate as many of them as humanly possible. The rest had to be
cleaned and frozen. Or canned. Canning happened at night because
it was too hot to do during the day, and it helped a lot if Dad was
home to pitch in. If everyone pitched in, it helped a lot.

The shadows slanted across the yard. The shadows slanted
across the garden. A horsefly droned past, on his way to somewhere
else. The barn swallows swooped and banked above the horse pasture. They spiraled, dove. Their forked tails.

One flew right between the legs of a horse. You saw it.

July also meant sweet corn. And sweet corn meant an electric fence,
which you turned on at sunset and it made a clicking noise like a
metronome. You could touch the wire between the clicks, but not
during the click. The click was the electricity, which reminded you
of the story of your uncle and how when he was a boy he had peed
on a long stalk of grass and the grass leaned over under the weight of
the pee and it touched the electric fence and then the electricity went
down the grass, then up the pee, and then . . .

Not a mistake made twice.

So, let's have corn for dinner. July. You go with Mom and cut fifteen ears. That's three apiece. The ears are medium-smallish, but that
means they're at their best—the kernels like translucent bubbles.
You husk the ears, then boil them, and then eat them with butter and
salt and hamburgers. The mess of it. The butter rolling down your
forearms and pooling around your elbows propped on the oilcloth.

A pitcher of iced tea in the middle of the table. One pickle in an
enameled bowl.

Then the nights of the corn harvest. Picking all the ripe ears. Big
buckets and bushels and tubs overflowing. The lawn chairs placed
in a circle. Piles of husks and silks, dumped onto the compost. It
overflows. The stories about our pet hen named June who used to

love corn shucking. You would shuck the corn and then hold the bare ear out to her and she would pluck off the little bugs and grubs quicker than quick, then she'd hurry on to the next person's corn. She was fast, fast, fast. And never once did her sharp beak break a single kernel of corn. That was June the hen, she who was born over the warmth of the pilot light. True, you had given her a bath when you were three, and she had been so sodden with water she couldn't stand up. "June wet, Momma. June wet." Mom blow-dried her.

After the husking, we moved inside, as the dark gathered on the lawn. Clean, cook, cut, package, label, and freeze. Corn for a year. Corn and more corn.

A steamy kitchen on a humid night.

Size-wise, the garden was like the house times four. To run a lap around the garden was a taxing event not to be undertaken lightly. It stretched from the horse arena, past the mulberry tree, and down to the fence around the chicken house. A gentle slope. There was the corn, of course, the peas, the tomatoes. Green beans, potatoes, sweet potatoes, beets. Sunflowers, radishes. Broccoli and cauliflower. Lettuce, carrots, and onions. Spinach. Marigolds at the row ends. Gladioli and zinnias. The asparagus bed. Rhubarb. Strawberries, raspberries, blueberries. Cucumbers. Lima beans and squash. Cantaloupes. Other stuff. Experiments. This summer, for example, there were watermelons, and we watched their vines spread out, and the melons started out like marbles lodged inside the blooms but got bigger and darker, and they were thriving and you would walk across the yard after dinner and kneel by the melons and when you picked one up it was still hot from the day. They were small, like cantaloupes, which was somehow disappointing, but when you cut into one it made a crackling, splitting noise and inside it was dark pink and warm and it had a better taste than any normal- or huge-sized watermelon you'd ever eaten, and you asked your parents, why didn't we grow these before? And the answer was, we don't know.

You could eat half of one of those melons by yourself and when you were done you had a shell like a cereal bowl and wished that you could actually use it as a cereal bowl or something, but that wouldn't work. It would shrivel by morning. Which was too bad.

Also, it was too small for a hat.

August. Already?

We gave the terrier a bath that summer. One bath. We filled a big galvanized tub with water, back behind the cellar house. The water was surprisingly cold. And then we found the terrier and picked him up. This in itself was a clear sign that something he didn't care for was about to happen. We put him in the tub of water and he jumped out. We put him in again and he jumped again. So we held his collar so he couldn't jump out, and we poured water over him and as his hair got wet he shrank dramatically in size until he looked like a burly rat. He was defeated and shivering and his eyes stared dully ahead and he didn't try to escape anymore. We soaped him up. Medicated soap, for the ticks. We tried to wash his face without hurting his eyes, and then we rinsed him and rinsed him. When it was done, we released him and ran away. We observed from a distance. In his state of defeat, it took him several moments before he realized he was free, and another few moments to figure out what to do with his freedom. Finally, he put his front paws up onto the edge of the tub, then hopped out and shook. Which was why we had run away.

The horses got multiple baths that summer, because Elizabeth rode them in a lot of horse shows. The horses stood still when she washed them. She hosed them down and then scrubbed and then hosed them again. That was the procedure. Elizabeth did the work—the horses were hers—but it was fun to watch. Or help a little. During the baths, the horses' bottom lips would go loose and floppy and they would get a dopey look in their eyes, which meant they really enjoyed getting washed. You could smell it in the air whenever one of the horses was getting a bath. It wasn't a bad smell. Also, there was a certain sound the water made when it was sprayed onto a horse. It almost sounded as if the horses were hollow. Or mostly hollow.

The horse trailer matched the pickup. It was a smart outfit. It was a nice trailer, but it didn't have any human living quarters in it. Our neighbors who moved away two years ago had a trailer that was half for horses, half for people, but ours just had space for two horses and some equipment. Still, you and Susan figured that the little compartment up front where you could store the tack would make a decent little sleeping compartment for a person. It could really make a pretty darn decent little cubbyhole for a sleeping bag, that's for sure. Especially for a kid-sized person. We sat in there. We would close the door, but not latch it, and sit in the dark. It was cozy, we thought, and would be a pretty good place to sleep. That's what we thought.

See Farther

I stood in the kitchen doorway, blinking. I was at Grandma and Grandpa's house, and Grandma was at the little kitchen table, writing. She didn't see me. Finally I entered and said good morning. She said good morning and got up and pulled out a chair for me, and I saw there was already a cereal bowl there, plus a spoon and the sugar bowl. At home, I wasn't allowed to have sugar on my cereal, only honey.

"You must have been one sleepyhead to sleep so long," Grandma said. She set the milk in front of me. She poured my cereal. She didn't pour quite as much as I wanted.

"What time is it?" I asked.

"It'll be ten thirty here in a bit." She poured the milk.

Ten thirty. I'd never slept that late in the history of me. At home, Mom would wake me up by singing a song called "Everybody Up." It was a song of her own invention.

Maybe it was the way Grandma had put me to sleep that was to blame. The routine was the same as ever. She read an animal story from a farm magazine and tickled my hair. But those stories were for little kids. A dependable raccoon and a troublesome duck. A lesson learned. Then she tucked me in so comprehensively that breathing was an exercise in tightness.

I hadn't thought that being ten years old would be like this.

I put more sugar on the cereal. "Why didn't Mom and Dad wake me up to say goodbye?" I asked.

"Oh, they wanted to get off early. They needed to pick up that beef before it got too hot outside."

Grandma was writing as she talked. She was writing in a little black notebook. A diary? Her hair was almost a perfect globe.

I thought about the beef. We had picked up a whole butchered cow last summer, too—one of Grandpa's cows—from the meat locker in Windsor. Mom had layered blankets and the sleeping bag in the back of the station wagon, then they stacked all the white paper packets of frozen meat in there and covered them with more blankets. It was a two-hour drive home, and every once in a while, Susan and I had put our hands back under the blankets to feel the cold.

When my cereal was gone, I pursued the layer of sugar at the bottom of the bowl. The wooden screen door banged on the back porch, and then the kitchen door opened and there stood Grandpa in his overalls—tall, sweating, holding his cowboy hat at his hip.

"Well . . . ," he said, looking at me. Then he breathed out through his nose.

I wished I hadn't slept so late.

"Well, looka who's up," he said.

"Me," I said. I rubbed my eye. It itched.

"Up and about," he said.

In the short time between breakfast and lunch—or dinner, as Grandma and Grandpa called it—I walked around the outside of the farmhouse. I investigated all three porches, each of which slanted or tilted in its own unique way. I knelt and looked under the side porch, and there, back in the darkness, I saw the curled, panting tongues of Ringo and Pal—the dogs. The front porch was loud because the air conditioner was set in the window blowing hot air onto the bushes. I walked out into the front yard and the sound of the air conditioner got quieter. There was one tree in the whole yard. I could see the garden across the driveway. Grandma was right: it was hot today. The grass was cut short, and it was largely dead, a casualty of the sun. There were two tractor-tire flower beds on the lawn, painted white. There was also the old swing set, which was smaller than I remembered. If you clutched one of its poles, it left white powder on your palm.

I sat on the back stoop, and Ringo and Pal emerged from their subporch den and lay in the strip of shade against the shed. They were filthy, and they looked at me not with Teddy's *what-are-we-going-to-do-now?* look, but with a sort of *what-are-you-going-to-do-now?* look.

There, through the gate, was the barn. Leaning.

It was too hot.

I went inside and Grandma gave me a popsicle and I went back outside and ate it on the back steps. This was where we always ate her homemade popsicles, and today it went particularly well because the heat was melting the popsicle quickly, which was how I liked it. I liked the popsicle to get soft so I could suck the juices out of it. But when the popsicle was gone I realized that what I'd just eaten was simply frozen orange juice. Not that I hadn't known it before, but today it sort of popped out at me. Frozen orange juice.

I went back inside. Grandma was making a cake. I stood near her.

"This is the first time I've visited you and Grandpa by myself, I think," I said.

"I think that's right," she said.

She talked a little about Elizabeth's birthday party on Friday—which was the occasion for the cake—then we started speculating how Susan and Elizabeth were enjoying their basketball camp in Warrensburg. She thought they were probably having a fine time of fellowship and sport. I added that Elizabeth would likely be the best player there.

When the cake went into the oven, Grandma asked me if maybe I wanted to paint and I said sure and she brought out the old box of watercolors that I remembered since forever and she put a margarine tub of water out for me and I wet the brush and then swirled it around on the orange lozenge of watercolor, raising a froth, and then Grandma reappeared with a brown paper bag and some scissors and I remembered that that's what one painted on here: cut-up brown paper bags.

On a brown bag, orange watercolor looked brown. Red looked brown, blue looked brown, green looked brown, and yellow—yellow just disappeared.

At sunset, I went with Grandma to water the flowers in the front yard. She gave me my own watering can with a spout shaped like a flower. As we watered I observed that the flowers looked thirsty and she said she was sure of it. We returned the watering cans to the back porch and then went to look at the garden. After that we carried two lawn chairs to the front yard and sat and waited for the stars to come out. We were facing the eastern sky and there was a gauze of gray at the horizon, and above that ran a long belt of reddish orange. Grandma asked me what color I would call it and I said extra peach. Ringo and Pal came and sat behind us. The sky got darker but there still weren't any stars and when a pickup passed we waved, and Ringo and Pal chased it. They trotted back toward us but didn't quite make it. They flopped down on the lawn between us and the road.

I sat cross-legged.

Across the road, a cornfield mounted its way toward the horizon. That was the direction Dad used to walk to school. A bit to the right, in the distance, the radio tower blinked.

Whenever my family and Uncle Kent's family were here in the summer, everyone would sit out on the front lawn of an evening and our cousin Brad would organize me and my sisters and his sister into a tumbling act. My best move was a somersault, but I could also leap variously. The girls could do cartwheels and Brad could do handstands, in addition to being the ringmaster. It had been a few summers—four?—since we had put on a good show out here.

We heard someone walking on the dry grass and we looked back and here came Grandpa carrying a lawn chair.

The stars did come. Grandma saw the first one.

The second day was hotter, and the third day the hottest yet. The thermometer on the side of the green shed said ninety-eight degrees when Grandma and I left for town. We cruised into Windsor.

Sunlight reflected off cars. It sure was a flat town. We stopped at the drive-up window at the bank but I was too shy to ask for a sucker and Grandma didn't ask and the teller didn't give me one. Maybe she didn't see that there was a kid in the car with Grandma.

We drove out the other side of town and I looked across the fields and the cattle were clustered under the few trees. I personally thought my suggestion that maybe my cousin-once-removed Craig might be lonely and might like to play with me this afternoon was a good idea. I had spent ample time with Grandma and Grandpa. Watching Grandma cook. Driving with Grandpa in the truck to buy feed. Stalking the cats. All of us going to the Wal-Mart and the Dairy Queen in Clinton. Supper in the church basement. I didn't have my bike with me or any other entertainment, really, and after lunch Grandma and Grandpa always both fell asleep sitting straight up in the living room and I would simply have to wait for them to wake up. We had visited the bookmobile yesterday. It stopped not far away in a place that was called a town and had a sign so you knew it was a town but really there was nothing there but two houses. I had picked out two armfuls of books but Grandma had not been sure if that was an appropriate number of books and so she asked me to put some back. The consequence being I ran out of books the same day. In Jeff City, the librarians knew we took home a whole big box full of books.

"I think the cows are hot," I said to Grandma. We were on a straight road.

"They can stand in a pond to cool off," she said. "If they have a pond."

"That's true," I answered. Our cows at home did that.

The car was slowing down, and Grandma made a turn onto another road. The car accelerated sluggishly.

"It seems flatter over here than at your and Grandpa's farm," I said.

"It's flat as a flitter."

"Is this the prairie?" I asked.

"Oh, I don't think people call it a prairie. That's more like Kansas."

I nodded.

"The farm I grew up on was just over there," Grandma said, nodding west, "and my brother—your uncle Emmett—used to call it 'Ruffin Valley' because it was so flat. He's a joker, just like you."

"What's Ruffin?" I asked.

"My family's name is Ruffin. I was a Ruffin until I married Grandpa."

"Oh." I thought. "Ruffin Valley. That is funny." I looked west.

"Sometime I'll show the old farm to you. You can't see it from here. It's where I was a girl."

I'd never put any thought into the idea that there was a place in this world where my grandmother had once been a girl.

"Is the house you grew up in still there?" I asked.

"You know, they bulldozed it. I guess so they could plant more corn. It was in a sad state, anyway. Would have made my mother weep to see how sad it was."

"When you were a girl, had cars been invented?" I asked. I thought it was a thoughtful question. It showed my understanding of history.

"I'm not *that* old," she said quickly. "There were cars," she said. "I'm not *that* old."

I felt bad. It was rare to see Grandma ruffled. She thought I had called her old. But wasn't she?

The real reason I'd asked to go over to Craig's house was that I was bored, and Craig lived in a brand-new ranch house on a big farm, and there was a pinball machine in the basement, not to mention other toys, including militaristic ones I wasn't allowed to have. But when I got to Craig's house, I felt bad about this play date and I watched Grandma drive away out the long driveway and then I watched her turn onto the blacktop and move farther and farther away while Craig, who I now remembered was too young and frenzied to engage in satisfying play, was talking nonstop and most of it was meaningless. Grandma's car faded into the haze.

"Hey, do you want to swim in the cows' watering tank?" Craig asked.

That night, Craig's mother, Linda, drove me and Craig into Sedalia, where we met Grandma, Grandpa, Mom, and Dad to see the State Fair Parade and a horse show. We got back to Grandma and Grandpa's house at eleven p.m. The next day was a whole day at the fair with Mom and Dad. As Dad said as we walked through the admission gate: "Let's hope it's not just a fair fair." It wasn't. Baby pigs sprinted around a little racetrack to reach a plate of Oreo cookies. Giant catfish and largemouth bass hung suspended in huge aquariums, just teasing us by their presence. A free pencil here. A free key fob there. Chickens in cages. Puffy chickens, fancy chickens. Big new tractors with tires as tall as Dad. We met Grandma for lunch at Wendy's. I got a glow-in-the-dark ball with my Kids' Meal, but I was scared of it because I'd heard that glow-in-the-dark things caused cancer. Grandma didn't eat much because she said her stomach had been upset in recent weeks. Back at the fair: a snow cone. A dollar to spend at the arcade. At the end of the day, my ankles were filthy with the dust of the midway. All of us went back to Grandma and Grandpa's again for the night.

Then, Friday, we picked up Elizabeth and Susan from basketball camp and went back to Grandma and Grandpa's for Elizabeth's seventeenth birthday dinner. Ham, rolls, scalloped potatoes, cauliflower with cheese sauce, green beans, iced tea, peach-whip salad, cake, and ice cream.

It was different with my family there. We sat out on the front lawn while it grew dark, and Susan and Elizabeth slumped in their chairs. I pulled on Susan's tan arm, but she wouldn't run with me. So I did some sprinting with the dogs. I rolled on the lawn. Far away, there was a line of clouds catching the last red of the sunset on their crowns.

I had spent the first part of the week trying to think of things to do, but anything worth doing involved having at least one sister around. That's the way it was at Grandma and Grandpa's. There was no substitute for a sister. On Tuesday, Grandma had bought me a set of string-connected walkie-talkies from the five-and-dime, and she even tried them out with me. But what were you supposed to say to Grandma over a string-connected walkie-talkie?

"Grandma," I had whispered conspiratorially from the top of the stairs, "I think it's time to take the cookies out of the oven."

This was doubly stupid because (a) it was stupid, and (b) the cookies had been baked hours ago. Plus, the walkie-talkies hadn't worked.

And now that my sisters were here, they were stubbornly lethargic. They didn't want to do anything. Yes, so I ran with the dogs by myself. I rolled by myself. I did somersaults by myself. I went and stood in the middle of the gravel road and looked one way, then the other, and then I looked back at my family assembled there in a line of lawn chairs. It was getting dark, and I couldn't tell if anyone was looking at me.

But in the morning I didn't want to leave. I wanted to feel the hot sun on the back of my neck and watch Grandpa driving the tractor across the field and listen to Grandma practice the organ in the cool, empty church and have her wash my hair in the kitchen sink.

You could see farther there. The sun was always out.

Stay

At the end of the summer, one night after supper, Dad and I drove to a state park named Bennett Spring. We checked into a little cabin and then walked to the edge of the big blue spring itself. The air smelled like cold rain, and suspended in the water were the dark-backed trout that had drawn us here. We'd never caught a trout, and not for lack of trying.

The air by the spring was cool, but as we walked away, the smothering heat of the day returned. Dad wiped his brow with a blue handkerchief.

"When I was your age," he said, "there was a drought so bad the grasshoppers ate the bark off the fence posts."

In the morning we were up early. Outside, the river was already lined with men holding long fly rods and wearing waders and fishing vests. What did they carry in all those pockets? Dad and I walked downstream with our beat-up spinning rods, our rubber farm boots clunking as we went, our lures rattling in Dad's big metal tackle box. Some of the fishermen watched us as we passed.

Along certain stretches of water, the fishermen were standing within arm's reach of each other. Beyond them, in the water, I could see the fish, all facing upstream, nearly motionless despite the current. In the middle of the night, hundreds of trout had been released into the stream: two trout for every tag that was bought yesterday. That meant there were two trout out there waiting for me.

Finally we found a place to stand. We waited, then the opening horn sounded, and the fishing began. Immediately, everywhere, fish were being caught. The dumb fish bit first. They'd never seen a lure in their lives. They'd lived in concrete tanks until today.

But the fish were not dumb enough. Or we were dumber than they were, because though over the next few hours we saw fisherman after fisherman leave with stringers of fish, we didn't have a solitary nibble. It was maddening because we could see the trout so clearly, we could put lures right in front of their noses, but they either ignored the lure or darted away. At home, on our pond, the bluegills would fight over our lures!

The stream grew less and less crowded, both with fish and men. We persisted, moving from spot to spot, casting, reeling in, casting, reeling in.

It started to rain.

I gave up on fishing and amused myself by teasing the small sculpins in the shallows with my lure. I dropped my jig near them and watched them dart out and try to bite the lure that was nearly the same size as they were.

After a while, I saw Dad talking to an older man. I went over.

"I'd stay if I had a slicker," the man was saying. "Good fishing in the rain."

"That so?"

"Puts them into a feeding mood. Plus they can't see you because the surface of the water is disturbed. So they're not as skittish." He smiled kindly at me. He looked at my lure. "I tell you, though," he said, "you might have better luck with this." He opened his palm-sized tackle box and took out a little brown lure with a silver blade. He handed it to Dad. "This is a fine spinner for trout."

We thanked him, and he went on his way. As Dad tied the new lure on his line, we decided to stay fifteen more minutes. Dad fished from the end of a concrete jetty. I went back to harassing the sculpins.

Pretty soon, Dad called my name. I reeled in my jig. It was time to go. I didn't want to leave, but I was also tired of staying. The return to the activity of not-fishing was essentially equivalent to the current activity of not-catching-fish. And I was soaked, and it was raining harder than before.

Dad called again. I looked. He was still at the end of the little jetty, and his fishing rod was bent down. At first it didn't even make sense—his fishing rod was bent, but why? What did that mean? And then I got it: fish!

A trout!

I ran over and arrived as he pulled a trout out of the water. It was a rainbow trout, which was like a piece of sky that swims and lives. We both looked at it in awe. He slipped it onto the stringer and held it up.

"I thought my hook was caught on a rock!" Dad exclaimed.

We went to the park store and bought another lure like the one Dad had. By the time we got back to the river, it was raining so hard we could barely see across the water. As far as we could tell, everyone else was gone. The rain was ours, the river was ours. Dad caught another fish. It flopped around in the shallow water, but he managed to get it onto the stringer. Then I hooked one, a nice one. Dad strung it before we took the hook out. We were grinning with excitement. Soon Dad landed another fish, but it slid from his hand and back into the water just as he unhooked it. He said, "Shoot!" and slipped on a rock and dropped his reel into the water. He pulled it out, dripping. At that moment I felt a quivering jolt on my line, and soon I'd pulled another trout into the shallow water. Dad lunged at the fish, but it wriggled out of his hands and flopped and flipped across the rocks, making slapping sounds. It was free of the hook. "Dammit!" Dad said as it slipped through his hands again. We chased it, but it finally shot off into the deeper water. The rain was a downpour. We were kneeling on the concrete jetty.

"I'm sorry, Jeremy," Dad said.

I shrugged. I wouldn't cry.

We had to leave anyway. We drove out of the valley. We were so wet, the car windows fogged up. I kept thinking about that last fish, having him right there but feeling him slip away. Then chasing him. Then having him again. Then slipping away . . .

By the time we got home, the skies were clear, and the temperature was back into the nineties.

Just two days later: school. Dew on the grass. Rambling tomato plants in the garden. The last bowl of cold cereal until May. Brushing my teeth in a hurry. Carrying a notebook fat with paper. Elizabeth, Susan, and I posed for a picture. Teddy sat at our feet, facing away from the camera. Elizabeth and I wore similar dark T-shirts, jeans, and white sneakers. Our hair was sun bleached, our arms tan.

"I guess this is the last first-day-of-school picture for Elizabeth," Dad said from behind the camera.

"Good," she said through her clenched-jaw smile.

Click.

We piled into the pickup and Elizabeth drove us to school— the route, as always, being more or less a tour past different cattle pastures. By the time we got to Russellville, it was warm. Inside the school, wading through crowds of kids we hadn't seen all summer, it was warmer. The heat was increasing. It was like we were migrating toward a volcano.

My new fifth grade classroom was tiny, no bigger than my bedroom. It had been the teachers' lounge last year. There were fourteen kids in my classroom. There were twenty-seven in the other fifth grade classroom. The grade school principal came by to say hello and explain that we were special because of our small room and that he, frankly, envied us. He didn't explain why. He was sweating through his suit. He clapped his hands together and repeated the thing about us being special, then he left. Our teacher, Mrs. Davis— young, pretty, a new teacher—watched him leave, then faced us. Just because we had a small room, she told us, didn't mean we couldn't have a more exciting, rewarding, and fun year than ever before.

I liked her.

Because our room had no storage space, we were each allowed to pick a locker in the hallway, just like the high schoolers. I picked locker 214—since fourteen was the number of Elizabeth's basketball jersey—and then Toni Renken casually picked a locker next to the locker that was next to my locker. In other words, the second locker to the left. Toni, whom I adored above all others. That Toni and I were in the same classroom for the third year in a row was a stroke of gorgeous luck. And that she picked a locker near mine . . . maybe she liked me—or still liked me? Anyway, there was something thrilling about it. We would build from the ground up.

The second day of school we were sent home with slips of paper announcing that for the first time ever students would be allowed to wear shorts to school. Until the weather cooled off. And only if the shorts reached all the way to the knees.

So come, September. Hold us in suspension. The glow of the summer becoming the gold of fall. The equinox. The equal nights. The harvest moon. The nests are abandoned. There is one nest lined with orange hairs from the horses' tails. Come, September. Suggest winter, but keep it at bay.

It was an evening to wish for, this first day of September, and after dinner Grandma and Grandpa went for a walk. The day's breeze was gone, and that along with the mild temperature accounted for the way they felt the air only while moving through it. It was refreshing. August was yesterday.

They walked south down the gravel road. The gravel on the road was white, with two smooth wheel tracks. There was corn to the left—taller than Grandpa—and pasture to the right. The sky was stretched wide and cloudless. There were crickets in the ditches.

Their footsteps made sounds on the crushed limestone road. They talked of moving the cattle to the southwest twenty. Of the likely shortage of forage this fall. They talked of how the choir would be visiting another church on Sunday.

They walked, talked, under the bluest of skies, past several blackbirds sitting on the power line.

Then, up ahead in the road, walking toward them, Grandma and Grandpa saw the Smiths, their neighbors. It was the kind of evening that drew couples out of their houses. The Jacksons and the Smiths waved to each other. And as Grandma raised her arm over her head, she felt—and remembered—two things at once: first, the hungry kind of hollowness in her stomach despite having just eaten, which had been pestering her recently, and which seemed related to the indigestion she'd been having for weeks; and second, the twinge of pain in her shoulder and neck—like arthritis, but sharper, denser.

The sun was down, but the light was holding.

So stay, September. Dwell. Stands of goldenrod listing in the sunlight. Sumac tinged with rust. The kingdom of apples. The realm of marigolds. Potatoes in the ground. Racks of onions drying on the front lawn. Walnuts fallen in the gravel road. A snakeskin, one piece, at the base of the rock wall. The way you can ride your bike to the top of the driveway—flanked by old cedars—then coast all the way down to the house, but never getting up much speed, never going fast at all, but coasting, comfortably, agreeably. Just coasting.

A Good Party

Mom stood near the top of the stairs—just her torso and head visible to me—and judged my room not yet acceptably clean.

"But I put everything away," I protested.

"You pushed your toys into a pile. You haven't made the bed."

It was Labor Day and we were off from school.

"Why do I even have to clean my room?" I asked. "I didn't invite Grandma here."

"Think about how many times Grandma has had your birthday at her house," Mom said calmly. "Think about how many cakes she has made you, even when it wasn't your birthday."

"I didn't keep count!"

Then Mom calmly appealed to my sense of responsibility and asked for my cooperation to make this a good day for Grandma. She didn't threaten punishment or raise her voice or anything. It was one of her most potent ploys. I had no weapon against it. She just asked for my help in this very adult way and then walked back down the stairs. I wasn't even sure why I was so mad. Perhaps because I saw no prospect of fun in the entire day.

Elizabeth was coming up the stairs.

"I'll help you, Jeremy," she said.

I was kneeling by the window, looking out. Elizabeth started making the bed. "Grab the other side," she said.

I got up and helped.

"It's a big birthday for Grandma," Elizabeth said. "She's seventy."

"I know," I said.

"When I turn seventy, will you throw me a birthday party?"

I laughed at such a ludicrous prospect. "Okay."

"I want lots of balloons and a lemon cake with a sugar glaze. Can you remember that?"

"By the time you are seventy," I said, "I will be too old to remember anything, so I will probably get you a chocolate cake instead. Or angel food, since that's what old people like."

We plopped down my pillows. We were done making the bed.

"Well, I'll be too old to remember what I asked for," Elizabeth said, "so I will eat whatever cake you put in front of me. Anyway, thanks for throwing me my seventieth birthday party."

"Yeah," I said.

"But for now, it's Grandma's day."

When the first car arrived—earlier than expected—I was the greeting committee. The car brought Grandma, Grandpa, Great Aunt Clarice, and Great Aunt Billie. I was enfolded by my grandparents and kissed. I wished Grandma a happy birthday and I offered to show her the ducks. Grandma said that she surely would be interested in seeing all those ducks she'd been hearing tell of. But before any organization toward such a duck quest could be mounted, two more cars pulled up, bringing Great Uncle Emmet; Great Aunt Rowena; Linda; Craig; Craig's older brother, Brian; and Grandma's cousin John D.

Our long kitchen table was covered with the pieced gingham tablecloth Mom had finished recently, and as soon as they walked through the door, Grandma, Clarice, Billie, and Rowena began cooing over it. The tablecloth was a patchwork of browns, reds, golds, and blues, each square about as big as a piece of toast. I had spent hours in the vicinity of the tablecloth's manufacture—sometimes playing under the kitchen table even as Mom was sewing on top of it.

"It's the first time we're using it, Mildred," Mom said. "In honor of your birthday."

"Oh, well, I . . . it's just wonderful."

I looked at the tablecloth and touched it. It *was* wonderful. I hadn't realized that before.

Then Grandma saw the cake and said, "Goodness gracious! That's a pretty cake. Did you help make it, Jeremy?"

"No."

"Now, Jeremy helped me do some baking while he was visiting us last month," Grandma said, "so I know how good he is at it."

"Is that so?" said Aunt Clarice. "Well, I'll swan. Do you want to be a baker when you grow up, Jeremy?"

I shrugged.

At each place setting there was a pint jar of our home-canned goods—either apple butter, peach jelly, or tomato sauce. These were favors for our guests. And the top of each jar was decorated with a little skirt of fabric and labeled with the name of one guest. That was how everyone knew where to sit. Grandma sat at the head of the table at the far end, which was the important place to sit. Usually that's where Grandpa sat. The windows and sunlit yard were behind her.

Us five kids sat at the card table in the study, and we could hear all the laughing and talking going on in the kitchen. Susan went into the kitchen for more rolls, but the adults said they were keeping all the rolls, and for some reason this made them laugh louder than they had laughed all day.

The cake was iced with whipped-cream frosting and had a drizzle of chocolate sauce that curtained down its sides. Mom had bought some new kind of candles—almost a foot long and about as thin as a strand of yarn—and we put all twenty of them into the cake and lit them. Despite their thinness, the candles burned with vigor, and as we sang "Happy Birthday" to Grandma—while I stood at her shoulder—what started as a flickering halo above the cake became something of a miniature conflagration.

"Oh, land sakes alive," Grandma exclaimed when it came time to blow out the candles. "Jeremy, help me blow these out!" I did.

It was a pretty cake, and we served it with "slices" of sherbet that Susan and Mom had made to look like watermelon wedges by freezing layers of sherbet in a bowl: lime for the shell, a thin layer of lemon, then watermelon speckled with chocolate chips.

In the living room, we sat around while Grandma opened her presents. We had secretly arranged for everybody to bring a funny "seventy" present. We gave her a soup mix made with seventy pinto beans, seventy navy beans, seventy lentils, seventy black-eyed peas, and so forth. Linda gave her a necklace made with seventy paper clips strung together. Each present made Grandma laugh more than the one before it, and she said that this was the best birthday she could remember. "I don't ever recollect having received such hilarious presents," she told us. "And, Linda, I'm thankful for the paper clips because I'm almost out . . ."

Finally, people headed outside to go see the ducks. Mom was finishing clearing the table. I was on the back porch, pulling on my rubber boots. Grandma had lingered in the kitchen. Everyone else was already outside.

Grandma offered to help Mom.

"I've got it in hand, Mildred. I'm not going to let you clear dishes at your own birthday party."

"Now, that was a fine meal—you put out a fine spread for us— and what with that cake and the ice cream that you and Susan . . . It's all sitting well—my stomach is having a good day. Been so touchy lately. I'm just really happy to have everybody here today, and all the planning and work you did . . . I appreciate it all."

"You're more than welcome."

"And we're all having a good time. Least I am!"

Outside, it had become overcast. We all walked down the hill to the pond, which had shrunk during the summer. The exposed shores were soft and stank of rot. Algae rimmed the water. It had become difficult to tell the baby ducks from the adults. They had grown up. I gave Grandma a full commentary: the saga of how one duck— given to me less than two years ago—had become forty ducks. How they nested anywhere and everywhere—in an old tire, on a pile of bricks, in a stump—and how we hunted down their eggs as a form of population control.

A little later, back at the barn, Elizabeth got out the horses, and a few of us rode them around while the older folks watched us and talked. Midafternoon, they got in their cars and left, all of them at once, and the five of us stood there at the end of the sidewalk, waving, and then we stopped. Our family. It had been a long morning getting ready, and it had been a good party, but now it was over. It went by fast.

the second part

In the Dark

As Grandma sat with the heating pad, she closed her eyes. Not because she was tired, but because it contained quiet comfort. It was a pause. She had been busy all afternoon with the usual town-Friday routine—groceries, hairdo, practicing organ at church—and the day had felt crowded to her, and pressed on her still. Also, there was the rest of the month to think about, the long climb toward Christmas: the shopping trip to Kansas City next week, the Neighborhood Club party here in only six days, Extension Club, Sewing Club, decorating and cleaning to do, wrapping presents, cooking, all of the cards to be written, the Cantata at the church. Finally, Christmas itself—the family here.

After a while with her eyes shut, she began to breathe more slowly. When the clock struck the half hour, she noted it but didn't feel rushed by it. Grandpa was still outside doing the chores. She heard the furnace cycle off and opened her eyes in time to see the sun suddenly coming through the low clouds. Those dull clouds had been overhead since dawn, but now the sun was below them, and she swiveled her easy chair to face the window directly—the south window in the living room. For a moment she looked right into the sun, and she remembered another sunset just like this, from another December.

Mother called for Mildred to fetch her coat and come into the kitchen. The day was cool but not cold. When she got to the kitchen, she watched Mother put two rolls—steaming from the oven—onto a tea towel and fold them up as if they were a gift. She handed the bundle to Mildred, then scooped a wad of butter into a tin cup and gave this to her, too. In the bottom of the cup, there was already jam.

"You know where Daddy's cutting up that tree?" Mother said.

"Yes."

"Here it's coming close to dark and I think it's taking him longer than he reckoned. So take these to him to keep him going until supper. Just go through the pasture and the gate should be open. All right?"

"The big gate?"

"That's right."

Outside, Mildred walked back past the barn and let herself into the pasture. The cattle were clustered by the doorway, and they watched her cross their field as if she were a creature they had never seen before. In her pocket, she could feel the warmth of the bread.

She passed on across the big pasture. The grass was still green there, and she thought about how it hadn't snowed yet this year. When she was in the middle of the pasture, she looked up at the sky, and the clouds seemed lower than they had all day. There had been no sun today, and she figured that if the clouds kept getting lower, tomorrow there would be no clouds at all, just a terrible fog.

The gate was open, like Mother had said, and she went through and followed the hedgerow all the way down to where it bent around the corner. There, lying in the grass, was the old bur oak that had been blown down last week. The ground had been wet and a wind had torn up the tree, roots and all. It had been one of the only trees on the whole farm.

"Daddy?" she called.

He wasn't there. His tools weren't there.

Many of the tree's branches had been sawed off and there was sawdust scattered about, and a pyramid of cut wood was stacked to the side. She walked around the tree and looked down into the brushy draw but there was nothing to be seen and as she turned back to the tree the sun came underneath the clouds and stunned her because it was so bright. She blinked and looked away.

She found a low branch on the fallen oak that was just right for sitting, and she looked back toward the house across the fields. The sun had brushed the land in a golden tone, and as she watched, the color deepened slowly and steadily until finally it burned like the last glow of a piece of coal, and only then did she realize the sun was setting—was nearly gone, in fact—and she didn't know how long she'd sat there.

Suddenly, there was Trixie, their dog, trotting through the last light, coming to her. Trixie, the good collie. Trixie walked up to Mildred and sniffed—she could smell the bread—and then sat down and waited.

It got dark. Mildred looked at her wet shoes but it was even hard to see them. She pushed her hair from her face. She liked the darkness and being alone here with Trixie, but she also felt too far from where she was supposed to be and she didn't understand how it had become night so fast. She had walked clear to the other side of the farm and was closer to Bryson, in fact, than to her own house. She thought of the schoolhouse not far away, which would be empty right now, and of her teacher, Mrs. Clay, and of her slate, and of the way her coat smelled when she put it on after school: it smelled like home. But when she put the coat on in the morning at home, it smelled like school. As if it knew where it was going.

Trixie stood up and looked into the night. She heard something. Then, after a little bit, Daddy said Mildred's name and came walking from the direction of the house. She couldn't see his face, but she could see the outline of his head—the tilt of it—and that was enough. He carried her home, and she could hear Trixie following them, and she didn't know how Daddy could see in the dark, but he could.

It was not the kind of memory that she had carried around for years and worn out with remembering and re-remembering so many times that it had stopped being a memory and turned into a memory of a memory. No, it was something she hadn't thought of in years— decades, even.

Her father had been a tall man.

Trixie had given many good pups.

Now, outside the window, the sunset was doing the same thing it had done that day when she was ten. It gave the open landscape a golden glow that faded and tarnished and deepened to orange, then to a color that was fragile and plumy—that old piece of coal, lingering. The shadows rose up from the roots of the grass. There were no lights on in the living room. When it was finally dark, the heating pad slipped off her shoulder and as she reached up to catch it, the pain came back—the clenched soreness across her shoulders and neck. She heard the screen door bang on the back porch. Grandpa was coming in. She leaned forward to get up, but it hurt too much, so she leaned back into the chair. She heard Grandpa come in the back door and click on the light in the kitchen. Then he padded through the kitchen until he stood in the doorway of the living room in his sock feet.

"'S dark," he said.

We didn't have the same glowering sunset that evening on our farm, just the blankness of night snuffing out a cloudy day. It had been the kind of dim day that didn't feel like day anyway, but like some outer province of night. We had an early dinner, and afterward Dad and I were excused from the dishwashing. We carried our gear to the car, then trekked across the barnyard. The calf named Kat was being weaned, and she'd been shut in a stall in the barn for a week already, bawling day and night for her mother. Now she went quiet when we came into the barn. From the shadowy corner of the stall, she watched Dad pour grain into her trough, and then she turned a circle—as if looking for an exit—and looked at the trough again. We turned out the light and left. As we reached the car, her woeful crying resumed.

We picked up my classmate Ryan Rutledge on the other side of Russellville, then continued out on Route C. I showed Ryan my new hiking boots and their tiny, zippered pockets, which, I explained, were big enough to hold two quarters each, or a fair number of movie tickets.

"Why?" Ryan asked.

"Why what?"

"Why would you put movie tickets in your boots?"

Outside Craig Linhardt's house, we gathered with the other Cub Scouts, and soon the coon dogs were let loose, and they milled among us, all noses and feet, and then all of us—dogs and men and a whole string of boys—went into the woods, following Craig's dad. My dad walked behind us, and in between the two dads was a total of seven Cub Scouts.

We walked through mud and passed black trunks of oaks and hickories. We each had our own flashlight, but even the most powerful of these barely penetrated the night. Craig's dad had a different kind of light—a hissing flame that bloomed from a silver reflector strapped to his forehead. This left his hands free for a rifle.

We stopped in a clearing of clumpy grass. The dads had us all turn out our flashlights, and we stood there in the dark, silent, listening to the baying of the dogs far away.

"Can you hear," Craig's dad asked, "how their pitch has changed? Like they're a little bit more excited?"

We resumed moving forward, listening to the dogs, following them, dodging low branches, trying to avoid brambles, splashing through soggy spots. We tromped onward, going around the side of this little hill, up that grassy draw, onward, onward. The night was moist but not foggy. I'd never been in these woods in the daytime, and so to traverse them at night was a strange introduction. We paused at a barbed-wire fence—a property line—and saw in the distance the light of a house.

But however fast or far we went, the dogs remained distant, which meant they had not treed a raccoon—or anything, for that matter—and were either chasing something elusive and fast, or were simply on the trail of nothing at all.

Eventually their baying became more scattered and halting,

and then we could hear that they were approaching us, and suddenly they appeared among us again and quieted, and one of them laid down, right there, and panted. Which is to say, the hunt was over.

At home, Elizabeth was on the phone. She wasn't supposed to be—not only was she grounded, but she should have been studying for tomorrow. That was the agreement she'd made with Mom. She and Mom had argued all through dinner about whether she could go to Catherine's house on Friday. But now she'd been thinking about Wayne, how he'd given her roses on Halloween, and how he'd been dressed up as a hoodlum, with his hair slicked back, and had looked even cuter than usual. And once she started thinking about Wayne, how could she not call him?

She'd been talking to him for half an hour when Susan opened the door to their room, saw Elizabeth on the phone, then backed out and closed the door.

"Shit," Elizabeth said. "Susan's going to tell Mom I'm on the phone."

Sure enough, within moments Elizabeth heard the kitchen extension pick up.

"Elizabeth, how long have you been on the line?" Mom asked.

"Five minutes."

"It's time to end it."

"Okay."

"I'm putting a one-minute timer on the microwave and when it goes off, that's it." Then Mom hung up.

"Good evening, Mrs. Jackson," Wayne said, knowing she was gone.

"This is a crock," Elizabeth said.

Exactly a minute later, Mom came on again. "Now!" she said.

"Okay!" Elizabeth said.

"I said one minute!" Mom said.

Then there was a clunk, and another clunk, a scraping sound, and a strange kind of chanting—like a two-year-old having a parade.

"What in the hell is that?" Wayne asked.

"I don't . . . oh . . . Jesus . . . ," Elizabeth said.

The kitchen phone had a twenty-foot cord between the receiver and the handset, and Mom was dragging the handset around the kitchen, like a dog on a leash, while chanting "Time! To! Get off the phone! Time! To! Get off the phone!"

When Elizabeth got down there, she was still doing it.

"I hung up, all right?" Elizabeth yelled.

Mom stopped. She put the phone back on the hook. The long cord contracted and coiled.

"Why'd you have to embarrass me like that?" Elizabeth asked.

"You broke our agreement," Mom said calmly.

"So? I didn't *kill* anyone."

"Being grounded means no calls."

"So ground me some more!"

Mom abruptly sat down on one of the kitchen chairs. Then her face changed. It turned red, it clenched. She started crying—and talking at the same time. "I don't know what I'm supposed to do!" she howled. "We had an agreement and that didn't mean anything to you! You wouldn't . . . I do everything! Everything! I cook everything, I clean everything, I do the laundry, I sew your clothes, and, I, and I, and you don't even listen to me—I'm in the dark with you—and I can't do it!" Then it was just crying. Under the bright fluorescent light of the kitchen.

Elizabeth stood there. She felt shame and heat. She set her jaw. Then she turned. She went back upstairs. She walked into the room she and Susan shared. She closed the door. She turned off the overhead light. She sat on the bed. Susan must have been hiding downstairs, because she wasn't here.

Elizabeth knew she caused Mom and Dad pain. She knew she disobeyed and broke curfew. And she felt trapped by who she was—the person who did those things, who hurt the parents who were so good to her—but she didn't really know how to change. She was a bad daughter.

She decided to study, to put her frustration into work. After a while, Susan came in and started getting ready for bed. They didn't say anything to each other. Susan went into the bathroom and shut the door. Elizabeth could hear her brushing her teeth. She thought about what she could say to hurt Susan—to get back at her for snitching—but she said nothing.

After nine, Elizabeth got up and went downstairs. Mom was putting away her sewing machine. Elizabeth got a glass of water and leaned against the kitchen counter. Mom was sweeping bits of thread off the kitchen table.

"I'm sorry about yelling," Elizabeth said. "And being on the phone."

Mom nodded.

"I don't mean to be so . . . mean," Elizabeth continued.

Mom went into the study. She returned and handed Elizabeth a piece of paper. Elizabeth read it. It was Mom's handwriting.

> *Ride On! Rough-shod if need be, smooth-shod if that will do,*
> *but ride on! Ride on over all obstacles, and win the race!*
>   —*Charles Dickens*

"That reminds me of you," Mom said. "You're a strong woman. And it's wonderful."

Mom had never called Elizabeth a woman before.

"But strength can hurt people," Mom added.

Elizabeth nodded.

They said goodnight, and Elizabeth went back upstairs. Susan was reading in her bed. Elizabeth washed her face, brushed her teeth, and took out her contacts. She sat down at her desk and copied the quotation into her journal. She wrote about the night. She finished, put her journal away.

"Do you want to read in bed for a little while longer?" Elizabeth said. "'Cause I do."

"Okay," Susan said.

"It's sorta early, but I want to get in bed, you know? And just read."

After the Cub Scouts' bewildering passage through the night, the lights inside Craig's house were startling and revealed a great deal more mud on us than we would have guessed. We'd brought extra clothes, of course, so we dumped our boots in the garage and were soon wearing clean, dry clothes.

After hot chocolate and snacks, my dad left, and Craig's dad and stepmother made themselves scarce, and his sister hid in her room—wisely—which left the house to the seven boys.

We created a sprawling sleeping-bag bivouac in the living room, and we watched a TV show, and played some video games, and then we challenged ourselves, as a group, to stay up later than we ever had—possibly even until dawn—and therefore draw forth all the rich marrow that the night had to offer. There was a hearty mood in the air, and we played a spontaneous game of hide-and-seek in which we were split into three teams. The game didn't work, but the confusion of it was fun, and during the fray we got interested in the basement, but a surprising late-night appearance by Craig's dad gently ended that excursion, and before long, one of us was asleep, then two were. So the grand alliance was failing, and one by one the Cub Scouts succumbed to sleep.

Then we were three: Craig, Jason, and me. We had plenty of things to say about the weak members of our group who were already asleep. We had plenty to discuss about the girls in our class. But in the middle of the conversation, we realized that Jason was no longer with us, so it was just me and Craig—the two survivors—and we engaged in cordial games of baseball on our handheld electronic game, whose red pinprick-sized LEDs signified fast balls and curve balls, base hits and home runs, strikes and fouls. Craig had been my ally since third grade—when we both discovered girls before the other boys had—and it was satisfying to know that we were the strongest of the bunch. We proved our staying power, and checked the clock at one point to discover that it was after two a.m., which was a respectable achievement, and we knew that we could stay up at least until four if we wanted to, and probably later. And on the one hand we wanted to, but on the other hand, we argued, what was the point? We knew we could do it, and we had proven our superiority, so who really cared? But we played awhile longer, because we could and because it was enjoyable. Then we decided: let's get some shut-eye. When this game is done. Ha. Double play. Inning's over. My turn. Must be after three o'clock by now. Gotta be. Don't even have to check the clock, because I know.

Grandma finally put on her glasses and looked at the clock on the dresser. 3:40. Well, I'll swan. Didn't that just beat all? She wondered if she'd slept at all. She had lain there, trying to put the pain away— put it elsewhere—but it hadn't worked, and now after looking at the clock, she heard the sounds of a light rain—that drip-drip in the gutters—and she decided to just get up.

So she sat with the heating pad on her neck, and she didn't even try to read or sleep. The doctor had put her on her fourth medicine for nervitis this week, and he'd said that if it didn't work there was another one to try, so she fully expected to be on her fifth medicine soon. On top of that, her stomach was still bothering her, and eating bran cereal every morning was like choking on a bale of hay. Didn't seem to improve matters either.

Grandpa had been helpful. He did all the driving now. He did the dishwashing. He couldn't be taught to cook, though. They'd lived well on leftovers recently, but those were dwindling.

The newest thing—and she didn't like to think about it—was that sometimes she couldn't turn her head. That's how much it hurt.

At about five o'clock, she went into the kitchen and laid out three Christmas cards to write. Just three. It hurt, but she did it— wrote them, addressed the envelopes—and when she was done she went back into the living room to wait for dawn.

Elizabeth actually woke up before her alarm and found that she was thinking about colleges. It was still pitch black outside, so she figured it was very early, but she checked her clock and saw it was only fifteen minutes before her alarm was set to go off. She rolled onto her back and looked at the ceiling. Susan was still asleep on the lower part of the trundle bed, a spray of dark hair across her cheek.

She ate breakfast. Mom came out of the study in her night-gown. Mom yawned.

"Did they catch a raccoon?" Elizabeth asked.

"No."

"Poor guys. But good for the raccoons."

As Elizabeth drove the truck to Columbia, daylight did come, but it was an even gloomier daylight than yesterday's—rain soaked, dull. She thought about Wayne, and being grounded. She thought about basketball. The Jamestown Tournament started Monday, and she wondered whether the team would actually play like a team instead of a loose affiliation of athletes occasionally interested in a common goal. Last year they'd had better ball handling.

The SAT took three hours. When she got back to the truck, the windshield was icy, but the roads—all the way home—were just wet.

After noon, Grandpa went to Warrensburg by himself. The weather didn't improve, but it didn't get worse, and when he got to the Christmas tree lot, there wasn't much of a selection. Was December 3 late for picking out a tree? He didn't like choosing one without Grandma. And the prices were higher this year. The one he got was a bit smaller than usual. Too broad and too short.

By the time he got home—about three—it was already starting to get dark.

Or: darker.

Stop

We brought the horses' tack into the house in the middle of that December, for winter storage, tucked it all into the study, and if you had been outside for a while and came back into the house, you would smell oiled leather—the English and western saddles, the bridles, the long loops of reins.

Our farmhouse was small. Upstairs was my room, open to the stairwell, and the girls' room. There was a right-of-way along the edge of my room leading to the girls' room. Inside their room, Susan and Elizabeth had separate desks and dressers, though they shared a trundle bed. They divided the room with a curtain of hanging beads. They had their own bathroom, with a little window that opened outward like a garage door swinging up.

Downstairs was the living room—underneath my room—and the study. The living room was the oldest part of the house, and a couple of long cracks in the plaster and a finger-wide gap in the floorboards showed that the room intended to separate from the rest of the house. We stuffed the gap with foam to keep the cold air out.

The study was the biggest room in the house, and it had the most roles. The walls were covered with built-in shelves that held hundreds of books from when Dad had been a student and professor. The room had the wood stove, which was a box of dark-green enameled iron with the enigmatic word "JØTUL" on the front. Two captain's chairs were near the stove. A built-in closet held Dad's suits and shoes. A tall wardrobe contained Mom's clothes. She also kept clothes in the cherry chest there. The study had a desk where all the business of the house was conducted. Behind the desk were built-in drawers and filing cabinets, and a tall built-in cabinet door that when opened revealed the house's circuit box and our fishing poles.

Along the study's western wall, in a bump-out, was a platform bed. In addition to everything else, the study was Mom and Dad's bedroom. The bed was situated sideways in the bump-out, and Dad slept on the inner section next to the three windows. That was the cold side of the bed in the winter. Mom slept on the near side of the bed. On the wall at the head of the bed was a swing-arm reading lamp. At the foot of the bed was a framed drawing of me as a baby, sleeping on my stomach with my arms and legs tucked under my body like a cat. Underneath the bed were wide drawers. In one drawer were rolls of wrapping paper, bows, spools of ribbon, labels, and folded sheaves of tissue paper. In another were topographical maps. Finally, underneath the mattress, near the windows, in the space not utilized by the drawers, there was a trapdoor that revealed a big storage nook—bigger than a bathtub—and there, in the cool darkness, we kept our canned goods. Applesauce, apple butter, peaches, pears, pear butter, tomatoes, tomato sauce, pickled beets, green beans, blackberries, blackberry jam, and blueberries.

The kitchen ran along the back of the house. We ate at a long table that had been made by Mom's great uncle in 1910. It could seat ten if it had to. There was a bathroom off the kitchen, and also the closed-in back porch where we kept our coats and jackets, baseball and softball bats and mitts, hats, gloves, keys, a rifle, my BB gun, boots, ponchos, tools, yardsticks, light bulbs, empty canning jars, a box of potatoes, the basketball, the collection of arrowheads found on our property, backpacks, pocketknives, binoculars, clothespins, a cistern pump, several house plants, flashlights, laundry supplies, old newspapers, empty egg cartons, the big freezer, the washer and dryer, and a box of clean and folded rags.

The house was painted white, the shingles were red, and the shutters were a glossy black. The floors were four-inch-wide southern yellow pine—long planes of orange wood that were knotless, smooth, and lustrous.

Me. Being in the bath. Slumping luxuriously. Wondering why fifteen minutes ago I had protested the Sunday night dip in the tub. Now that I was here, there was nowhere else I wanted to be. I turned off the water. It was up to my navel. I listened. I heard Susan practicing piano. I heard the desk chair roll briefly across the wood floor in the study. Then I heard the door of the wood stove being opened. Then shut.

I soaped, I shampooed. Wet hair made me cold, so I turned the hot water on full blast for a bit, then adjusted it to the hottest drizzle possible—a drizzle to maintain an appropriate overall temperature. A companionable drizzle. I dipped my washcloth in the hottest water—beneath the spout—then draped the cloth across my back like a cape. A sheet of warmth.

Same washcloth, a few minutes later: take your hand and imagine you're holding an apple, palm up. Drape the washcloth over this framework. Gently lower your hand into the water, using your other hand to keep the cloth's edges from floating loose. Notice that the cloth has filled with air. Gather the edges of the cloth together and clench them shut, thus trapping the air. This was a washcloth bubble.

Which could be: submerged without losing any air; held out of the water and touched very softly without losing any air; submerged and pressed lightly to create small tickling bubbles; submerged and pressed moderately or suddenly to create a rush or explosion of small bubbles; or any combination of these things, within reason, until the bubble was deflated.

Some minutes later—clean, clad, and warm—I lay on my back beneath the Christmas tree, looking up into the branches. Squinting transformed the Christmas lights into fractured stars. Last week, all five of us had gone and cut down this tree—a healthy and fragrant cedar—from the little field between the mailbox and the deep woods. I had made it my job to decorate the very lowest branches of the tree, even the innermost hidden regions, and I was enjoying revisiting my handiwork right now, after my bath.

Then I heard something.

"Hey, listen," I said.

"Don't bug me," Susan said. She was still practicing piano, just a few feet away.

"No, listen." I pulled myself out from under the tree and sat up. "I hear Tracks."

Susan stopped playing and we both listened. The house was quiet. There was wind outside. Finally we heard the tiny noise of our black cat.

On the back porch, we flicked on the light over the back stoop and leaned as close to the window as possible. There she was, below us, meowing.

We let her in and she talked to us loudly—thanking us—as she walked into the dark kitchen. We followed her on hands and knees and gave her some milk, and when she was done lapping, she sneezed daintily. Then she walked away and we followed, still on hands and knees, and she passed through the living room and looked at the Christmas tree and we were hoping she would play with the ornaments that dangled from the lower branches—bat them around like she had a few days ago—but she kept going, entered the study, and walked right up to the wood stove. The heat there was tremendous.

I couldn't resist touching her, and I pulled her toward me, but that wasn't fair, so I let her go, and we sat still and let her choose which lap she preferred. We also agreed that if she didn't choose one of our laps, then we were not allowed to force her into one. On this particular night, after a bit of grooming, she chose my lap, even though she was technically Susan's cat, and I leaned over her huddled form and put my nose in her fur and inhaled. She smelled like the hayloft. She'd been sleeping in the barn. She purred.

Mom was reading on the bed. Dad was at the desk.

Dad wrote check number 3005 for forty dollars and no cents to Dartmouth College. He wrote check number 3006 for thirty-five dollars and no cents to Cornell University. He looked up at us.

"I don't know how you can sit so close to the stove," he said.

"I like it," Susan said.

"Tracks is asleep," I whispered.

Meanwhile, upstairs, Elizabeth was writing a college application essay at her desk. She started a new paragraph. Her ink was blue.

Many people don't realize this problem exists, she wrote. *They believe,* she wrote. She paused. She thought. She wrote, *their actions*—

Susan and I walked in.

"I'm toiling here, people," Elizabeth said.

"We're just gonna look at our Advent calendars," Susan said.

"Do it in Jeremy's room."

Susan got her Advent calendar from her dresser.

In my room, we didn't turn the light on. We sat by the open stairwell. The lights from the Christmas tree lit up the stairwell with a patchwork of colors—apricot, green, blue.

My Advent calendar was a snowy town scene. Carolers, dogs running amuck, candles in windows, that sort of thing. It was a good Advent calendar; it was not great.

Susan's Advent calendar was from four years ago, and it was our favorite. It depicted a huge oak tree and all the animals that lived upon, below, and inside it. The rabbit and hedgehog tunnels were marvelously cozy. A fuzzy owl sat on a limb. The moon cast shadows of squirrels carrying nuts tied with bows. There were other tracks in the snow, some of them leading to flaps that had yet to be opened. Now we closed all the flaps and reopened them one by one—up to and including today's door. We speculated about what would be hidden behind the remaining doors.

"What about here?"

"The cupboard? I think there will be food in there."

"Maybe some honey."

"I remember there was a little jar of jelly somewhere."

"Oh, yeah."

"And the lid was open and there was a spoon stuck in it."

"That's right. I forgot that."

"Whose kitchen is that, anyway?"

"The rabbit family, there."

"I wonder how late it is there. How late at night."

"There aren't any clocks . . ."

"Look, that's the smallest Christmas tree ever. A mouse Christmas tree."

"It's probably just a sprig that fell off a real Christmas tree, and they took it and made it their tree."

"Yeah."

"I like that old rabbit asleep in that rocking chair."

"Yeah."

"She's a grandma."

The next morning, we three kids piled into the pickup truck and tooled out the driveway. Teddy, as usual, chased us all the way to the pasture gate. I turned around and looked out the rear window as Teddy trotted back to the house. He was a good dog, and his short legs had a lot of chase in them.

When we came down the driveway's little hill and swung around the corner, we saw something in front of us at the far end of the long flat stretch, where the driveway met the road. Something red.

"Oh, man," Elizabeth said.

"A stop sign!" I said.

"As if Mom and Dad aren't mad at me already," Elizabeth said. But we all laughed. We all knew who had done it: Wayne Elwood.

Elizabeth stopped the truck at the stop sign. "No one can blame me," Elizabeth said. "I didn't tell him to do it." The sign was a bit crooked, and a bit tall—it hadn't been planted deep enough.

"Well, you are the one who needs more stop signs," Susan said. She'd seen to the root of the joke. Elizabeth, after all, had come to be known as "Crash" Jackson because of her wrecks and mishaps. A week after getting her license, she'd rolled the truck at sixty miles an hour and walked away unharmed. (You could still see the twelve new fence posts that replaced the ones she plowed through.) Soon after that, she'd had a parking lot run-in at the funeral of her ag teacher. A fender bender at a funeral, of all things. Then there was an incident on Missouri Boulevard in Jeff City that left the truck's flank all scraped up. Next there'd been the storm that had damaged the windshield and paint. So the joke was simple: Elizabeth was a bad driver and needed more stop signs.

Ah, Wayne Elwood! He was, as far as I was concerned, a paragon of coolness: his smirky smile, his scruffy sneakers, his ruffian good looks, his ability to do backflips and climb anything. Not to mention his talents behind the steering wheel. For example, one time he left a spectacular series of fishtails in the gravel down the entire length of Mount Hope Road. And once I had been in his car with Elizabeth and he'd lit a bottle rocket with his cigarette and then aimed the bottle rocket—still holding it! and driving!—at a crow sitting on a power line, and the rocket whizzed out of his hand and popped right under the crow's tail and the crow left in a flurry of black feathers. And Elizabeth told Susan—after swearing her to secrecy—who then told me—after swearing me to secrecy—how she'd been hanging out with a bunch of the guys at the bridge on Rockhouse Road—a long, one-lane, iron-truss bridge dating from 1907 that spanned the Moreau Creek about seventy feet above the water—and someone, some older guy, had offered anyone ten dollars to climb the bridge's framework. Wayne had pulled away from Elizabeth and scrambled up the narrow, rusty endpost, walked the length of the bridge's high, arching top beam, had come down the other side, returned to the group, and then refused the money.

Drunk, of course.

We Had Some Lights

There was a certain hat, of a certain brand name, in a certain store, in the mall at the edge of Jefferson City, that I saw, touched, tried on, and desired. It was a hat that was not within my means, but it was clearly a special item, and would significantly elevate the status of whoever wore it. Described briefly, it was a white cotton hat of a flat-topped baseball style, with a black checkerboard pattern ringing the lower half of the crown, a small, two-initial logo on the front, and a black bill. It was a simple thing. It was beautiful and complete.

I spoke of this hat at school, casually, as if it would soon be mine, and no one knew what I was talking about except a girl who was new to our class. Her name was Kathy Smith, and she was not from around here, and she knew a lot more of the world than my other classmates did, and recognized not only the brand name of this particular hat, but even knew exactly what it looked like. More important, she knew what this hat meant. She knew that it was special, that it signified a certain order of coolness that stood above most anything we knew, and that I certainly should obtain it, because it befitted me.

Where had she sprung from with her blond hair, her attitude of power, her knowledge of hot tubs? She was cute. She rode the same bus as I did. She sat with me, nudged her hip against mine. She employed euphemistic language in the service of explicit suggestions that I did not completely comprehend. At other times, she was direct: I was the cutest boy in the class, she said.

I told her stories. Funny stories. I made things up. I would someday, I told her, invent suction cups for your feet so that you could walk on the ceiling. She said I was funny. She laughed early and often. She smiled gleamingly.

The hat would be mine.

I considered adding the hat to my Christmas list, but that would mean waiting a month for it. My own cash reserves barely topped two dollars, and this left me with little recourse but to plead my case before the Court of Mom. At first, this yielded nothing, but I was persistent and levelheaded—two things I knew would impress her—and the next time we were at the mall, we went back to the store with the hat and I showed it to Mom. She understood it was something I truly wanted, and she explained to me that when there was something that we wanted, we had to make sacrifices in order to get it, and work hard, blah blah blah, and therefore earn what we wanted. She also invoked the whole *want* versus *need* issue. I had heard this kind of baloney many times from her. It was a dead end. So I had to force the issue. Right now, right here. I pointed out that I had two dollars, and that if she would pay for the rest of the hat I would reassign my allowance for the month of December back to my parents, thus paying off the debt. This would leave me penniless in December. Penniless, but hatful.

We were having this conversation standing in the store, in front of the round rack of clothes, on top of which sat the hat (one hat, whereas before there had been three). Mom picked up the hat, looked at it again, and had me try it on. She accepted my proposal. We paid for the hat. Eight dollars. For a hat! Eight dollars, forty-one cents. Tax! I had forgotten about tax, which meant that part of my January allowance would be docked, too. But that hardly mattered.

The mid-December week that started with the stop sign at the end of the driveway also brought the first snows of the season. There were a couple of inches on Tuesday. More on Thursday. The two tall windows in our little teachers'-lounge classroom fogged up at the edges. The radiators clicked and clanked, putting forth more heat than we needed. By Friday, there was enough snow to move recess inside—a profusion of soft, red rubber balls being flung recklessly about the cafeteria. The smell of lunch, back in the kitchen, almost ready.

Chili, carrot sticks, one packet of saltine crackers, half a peanut butter sandwich, fruit cocktail, sugar cookie, milk.

Elizabeth drove us home from school. The house was empty, and already it was getting dim outside, so we turned on more lights than necessary. We plugged in the Christmas tree. We turned up the heat. We let in the cats. There was a note from Mom telling us to get a few things out of the freezer to thaw. She also suggested a couple of ideas for snacks. Suggestion one: grapes. We looked for grapes. Couldn't find them. Suggestion two: peanut butter and crackers. Had she not paid attention to our lunch menu? We'd already had peanut butter today.

Susan fetched the things from the freezer while I lugged the little black-and-white TV out of the sewing closet. It was our only TV, and we were allowed just one hour of television a week, but because Mom wasn't there, and because I was feeling rebellious in my still-new hat, Susan and I settled down for some sitcom reruns. We put the TV on the kitchen table and were barely ten minutes into a sitcom when we heard a car and scrambled to put the TV away. Susan fled upstairs, leaving me in the kitchen wearing my cool hat, watching Mom come up the back sidewalk, as Grandma and Grandpa pulled up in their car behind her.

Mom slid groceries onto the kitchen counter and said hello to me.

I said, "We couldn't find any grapes."

"I'm sorry, I remembered only once I got to the store that we were out. But I bought some and I'll wash them for you in a minute."

Grandma and Grandpa were making their way toward the house.

"Aw, man," I whined, "they're going to *kiss* me, aren't they?"

Mom laughed. We didn't kiss each other in my family, but Grandma and Grandpa kissed us right on the lips. There was no way around these kisses. They were obligatory.

And then my grandparents were inside, in the kitchen, and greeted me, and I greeted them sourly, and Mom promptly related to them exactly what I had just told her about them kissing me. They thought it was funny. And then they proceeded to kiss me anyway.

Grandma leaned down and planted one on me, and the bill of my marvelous hat bumped into her forehead.

"Whoops, nearly knocked your hat off, didn't I?" she said.

I straightened it. "Yeah."

"I've never seen a hat like that," she said.

"It's new," I said. I told them the brand name.

Grandpa said, "Wearing a hat inside?" He shook his head in disapproval.

Mom picked up the school papers I'd brought home. One was the new edition of our classroom newspaper, the *Davis Press,* named for our teacher. Mom gave this to Grandma to read while she and Grandpa were sitting in the living room, but I looked in there after a minute and saw that though she was holding the sheet of paper on her lap, her eyes were closed. Grandpa's eyes were closed, too. Mom saw me looking and said something about how tired they were from Christmas shopping in Jeff City. She assigned me to start a fire in the wood stove, and I said sure, and I went into the study and opened the door of the little cast iron stove and there was a cool darkness inside and the soft sound of the wind blowing across the top of the chimney, far above.

A few hours later, the gymnasium lights went down—row by row—and the crowd hushed and all was dark except for the stage lights, and then there came Mrs. Meyer, to tenuous applause, and she welcomed everyone and said that all the children had worked extra hard this year and she knew the audience would enjoy the program. Just minutes ago, when I'd come in the front door with Mom, Grandma, and Grandpa, Mrs. Meyer had gotten up from the ticket desk and hugged Grandma. They'd known each other since long ago.

The sixth grade band started off the program with two songs, wavering, wobbling, with percussion so precise and loud it served only to highlight the general incompetence of the other players.

Then the kindergartners took to the risers onstage, and lo! how the flashbulbs popped in the dark volume of that hall. Then the program ascended through the grades until it was our turn to sing

"Marshmallow World." Onstage the lights were blinding, and Craig Stubinger hadn't gone to the end of the riser, so the second row was all bunched up. Prodding ensued. Mrs. Meyer was below us, on the gymnasium floor, banging at the piano while standing and conducting us by bobbing her head and mouthing the lyrics in an exaggerated manner. She looked even smaller than usual down there. When the song was over, the boys filed offstage. The girls sang "A la Nanita Nana"—a slew of Spanish nonsense—then the sexes reunited for "Silver and Gold." Done! We marched away, relieved, listening to the applause trail off.

"That was a really grand show!" Grandma exclaimed as we walked up the empty elementary hallway toward the side lot where we'd parked. "A real showcase of wonderful holiday music!"

"Thanks," I said flatly.

"I think that you all kept real good time and had a lot of spirit, and I was just sure I could hear your voice above all the others, steady and bright."

"Jeremy!" someone called from behind. Here came Kathy Smith, jogging up to us. "This is for you," she said, and handed me an envelope and then slipped away without saying boo to the adults. She had a way of doing things.

I looked at the envelope. *To Jeremy,* it said in the top left-hand corner. *From Kathy,* in the middle. And in the lower-left corner was an illustration of a unicorn under a rainbow, surrounded by roses, two birds, two butterflies, and fluffy clouds. On the unicorn's forehead, beneath its horn, was a red heart.

"Now who was that?" Grandma asked.

Mom explained that Kathy was new to our class.

On the back of the envelope, in a lovely neon yellow, Kathy had written: *Merry Christmas.*

"Is she your sweetheart?" Grandma asked.

I shrugged and shook my head at the same time.

Mom said, "I think she wants to be."

"What happened to that little redheaded girl?" Grandpa asked. The little redheaded girl had been my girlfriend in kindergarten, to

the extent that there was any such thing as a girlfriend in kindergarten, but for some reason Grandma and Grandpa just wouldn't let
go of her.

"I don't know," I said.

Grandpa laughed at this in his way, which was to blast out one big
"Ha!" He paused, said, "You don't know?!" and then did another "Ha!"

In the parking lot, we said goodnight to the grandparents. They
would drive back to Windsor from here.

At home, I opened the note from Kathy. The stationery matched
the envelope. Kathy's handwriting was a very adult-looking cursive,
even if it did sometimes slant left.

> *Dear Jeremy*
> *Call me I really*
> *want to talk*
> *to you and I promise*
> *I won't loose my temper*
> *please Call me*
>
> *Love Kathy*
>
> *PS Please*

It was complicated, this. It was troubling. I felt bad about the whole
thing. On the one hand, it was exactly like I wanted it to be—I wanted
girls to pass me notes on unicorn paper with neon-pen greetings on
the back. Sometimes, she even included a nice sticker or two on her
notes. We shared a love of stickers. She was a master of these elements.

But I wanted to break up with her.

Grandpa drove through the night, and they got home after the news
was over.

Grandma sat up and read until after twelve. She didn't feel well
and was worried she wouldn't sleep, so she read and thought about

the trip to Jeff City and the music program, and she listened to the house contracting around her as the night grew cold. She went to bed, had a poor time of it, rose before five and soaked in a hot bath—to no relief—then put on her robe, worked on her nails, wrote a grocery list and yesterday's diary entry. Even this small amount of writing worsened the pain in her shoulders by many degrees.

It still wasn't dawn. She sat in the living room in the flowery chair near the furnace vent. This chair was softer on her shoulders and neck. On the table beside the chair was the music program from last night. She read through the titles. There was also the "newspaper" from my classroom. She read all eight articles, which fit on one side of one sheet of paper. The articles were: "The Poster Contest," "Scoliosis Screening," "Business Letters," "Ice Cream Cones," "Jennifer Meisel's Birthday," "The Door Decoration," "Math Division Races," and "Decorating the Tree."

She noted that I'd won both the poster contest and the door decoration contest, but it was the last article she liked the best.

```
Decorating the Tree
     By Travis Wunderlich
We decorated our tree December 15, 1983.
Jimmy brought the tree. It is a little tree,
but it is pretty. We have lots of decorations
on it. It has lots of bulbs on it and ice cream
cones too. We had some lights. When the
teacher tried them out they worked, but when
she put them on they did not work. But she
had some green lights, they worked.
Jimmy and Mitchell had to get a can of sand
for it to sit in. We finally got it up.
```

She read it twice, and smiled both times.

Coming Home

Grandpa woke early. He could tell by the way the frost had crept up the inside of the bedroom storm windows that it was as cold as they'd predicted, if not colder. He'd been thinking about the cows since yesterday and even felt like he'd been thinking about the cows while he'd been asleep, but he hadn't come up with any ideal solutions, and the fact was that when the temperature was below zero, there was no such thing as an ideal solution.

It was still dark outside, but because of the snow from yesterday—plus a bit more overnight—the landscape was white and bright and he could see easily. He was bundled well—layers and layers—but as soon as he stepped outside the air chiseled its way in at the seams and gaps. He walked to the shed, brushed snow off the thermometer. Minus ten. Gracious. Goodness gracious. He walked out the short driveway to the gravel road. The road was covered with snow and rutted with wheel tracks. He kicked at the snowy road with the toe of his insulated rubber boot, and the snow yielded nothing. Might as well be concrete. He had been surprised that the Christmas Cantata at church hadn't been canceled yesterday. But everyone had made it, and afterward the Youngs' house was packed for the party. It was full of people. It was hot. There was a huge fire in the fireplace. The kind of fire you could hear across a room full of people. He and Grandma had driven to the program in the truck. Four-wheel drive. Creeping along. In the Cantata, she had played well. She always played well. She sat straight and proud on the organ bench, wearing her white choir robe with the red trim, and she smiled when the music was done. She wanted to go to the party, and at the party she was bright and full of energy. Talking. Laughing. But he knew she was in pain.

Grandma and Grandpa had two farms: the home farm—where they lived—and the farm called LBJ (an acronym that was a hybrid of Lizzie Brown, the aunt who'd originally owned the farm, and Jackson). The farms didn't connect, but they did nearly touch at the corners, like two black squares on a checkerboard. LBJ was to the southwest of the home farm. Most of Grandpa's row crops were at LBJ: milo, soybeans, corn. Each autumn, he took the cows there to let them clean up the fields after the harvest and take any late grass they could find. They liked the woods there, too. This year he'd taken the herd to LBJ just after Thanksgiving, and now they needed to come home. They'd gleaned what they could, but now the snow had ended their grazing. He didn't have an easy way to get hay bales to them there. Plus, with these temperatures, the pond and creek would freeze so solid it would be nearly impossible to keep them in fresh water. Of course, it would be hard on the home farm, too, but at least it would be closer. He'd walk out and chip through the ice on the pond twice a day.

He didn't want to ask for help. Not on a day like this. It was too cold. Normally, with Grandma using the car to block the road in at least one place, he could run the cows east along the gravel road from LBJ, then turn them north for a mile, get them past the house, barn, and garden, then head them into the pasture. He, Grandma, Smith or another neighbor, maybe a boy or two. Didn't take long. The cows sort of knew the routine, anyway. They got excited because they figured they were moving someplace good, someplace with fresh grass. They knew to follow. It was the calves and yearlings that were the problem. They didn't know what was going on. Didn't trust you. Were fast. They'd outflank you.

It was his own fault. He should have moved them on Thursday, but just didn't think it through, and Grandma really needed his help with decorating and wrapping. Should have moved them on Friday, but they'd gone up to Jeff City and to the Christmas music program. And then Saturday he'd driven Grandma into town for her appointments, and he'd had a sore throat to boot, and when he finally got home, he discovered that the truck had a low tire, and then he just ran out of daylight. Of course, Sunday was the storm, and church, and the Cantata, and the party. Plus, he didn't work on Sunday unless he had to.

So that's how he got here, to Monday, with windchills in the negative thirties, with flurries in the air, with the cows needing water and hay, and dawn still not here. And his plan to move all sixty-one head back to the home farm by himself was far from perfect, but he would go ahead with it. Instead of running the cows home the long way around by the road, he would try to lead them across the short gap where the corners of the two farms nearly touched. Between the northeast corner of LBJ and the southwest corner of the home farm ran Larry Womble's long driveway. So he would let the cows out of the old gate at the corner of LBJ, run them along the driveway, and then head them into the southern part of the home farm. He would block the driveway with the tractor at one end and the truck at the other so they'd be able to go in only one direction. There were fences on both sides of Womble's driveway, so really there'd be no place for the cows to go except to the home farm.

He got into the truck. He didn't have the key. He went back inside, got the key from the kitchen. Back outside, the dogs were waiting by the truck, watching him. Pal was shivering. Grandpa got into the truck. Started it. He got out, locked the front hubs. He brushed the snow off the windshield. Got back into the truck. It was good to be out of the wind, but there was a different kind of coldness inside the truck. A metallic coldness. The smell of cold dust.

He drove down to the barn. He loaded two hay bales into the back of the truck, then headed down the road. He could hear individual teeth of the gears turning in the transmission. So cold. Lights on in the Smith house. He kept going, turned west, crossed the railroad tracks, pulled up to the LBJ gate. He got out, unlatched the gate, dragged it open through the snow. Got back into the truck, drove through, got out, closed the gate, latched it, got back into the truck, went on. The cows weren't in the front field. He crossed the creek, frozen solid, passed the old, abandoned house. The cows weren't in this southern part of the farm. He went farther, then saw them, out across the open fields, way over on the west side. Way over there. He drove toward them across the frozen ground. They heard him coming and looked up. He drove closer so they could see and smell the hay. He stopped near them and let a few of the cows come close to the truck. Then he drove east, to the far northeastern corner of LBJ, unloaded the hay bales, cut the twine that bound the bales, then kicked the hay to spread it around.

He opened the gate there, drove through to Womble's driveway, got out, closed the gate. He could see the cows coming across the field. They were headed for the hay.

Womble's driveway used to be called Uncle Charley's Lane. All this land used to be in the family. That's why there was a gate here in the first place—between LBJ and Womble's driveway. He drove east down the driveway, and after about fifty yards he was at the south-western corner of the home farm, and there was another old gate. He got out, cut the rusty wires holding this gate shut, and opened it. Probably hadn't been opened in ten years.

At home, he called Womble. It was 6:41.

The phone rang twice.

Grandpa said, "Larry, it's Belford."

"Eh, mornin'," Larry said.

"Hope it's not too early, I know you leave early, and I wanted to catch you in."

"It's not too early."

"Sure having some patch of bad cold."

"That's for certain," Womble agreed. "Had a pipe freeze last night. Awful mess."

"Larry, I've got the cattle over on the LBJ and I shoulda moved 'em home last week but I missed my chance, and now, now I've got to do it today, so I thought if I could run them down your lane there, it would make it easier."

"That's fine, Belford. You got it in hand?"

"Oh, sure. They'll do it. They'll go."

"Cold day to be out. I'm leaving in ten minutes or so, or . . . but . . . if you need help, I can stay. Block the lane for you."

"No. I'll just use the tractor. That's all right. They'll do it."

After he hung up, he took his handkerchief out of his back pocket and blew his nose, then realized he was hot from standing inside for just this short time, bundled up so. The house was still. He went back outside. He shoveled the sidewalk. Cleared the snow off the back stoop as best he could. He heard a soft purring and looked around the corner of the house to see Womble's car driving up the road. Too late to wave. But now he could get to work. Daylight was rising. Cloudy daylight. He was hungry.

To drive a cabinless tractor in such weather was simply a way of magnifying the windchill, and he stopped twice on the short jaunt down the road just to readjust his collar and scarf. He turned into Womble's lane, which turned him into the wind, and he could feel the heat of his body being sapped away—not just his nose and fingers and the cold spots where his wrists passed between his sleeves and his gloves, but also his thighs, his head, and his torso. His eyes watered in the stinging breeze, and tears ran from the corners. He wiped them away, but they had already partially frozen on his cheeks.

He parked the tractor just to the north of the old LBJ gate. He wedged it in diagonally and lowered the front loader, blocking the lane. He walked to the LBJ gate. He leaned over the gate, looked at the herd. They'd eaten all the hay already, and some of them were drifting south, on the move. He called them. A few looked. They weren't as close as he'd thought they were. He called again. His voice wasn't carrying. And it was time to move on. He walked out Womble's driveway, then up the road to the house.

He got into the truck. It was hot in the cab; he'd left the heater blasting. He wanted to sit there and just warm up for a little while, but there wasn't time. He drove to the barn, got one more bale of hay. He drove down the road again, listening to the radio. There were reports of bad weather, more to come, and Christmas was just a week away—no, six days. Six days.

Back in Womble's driveway, at the corner of LBJ, the herd was waiting. They were waiting as if they knew the plan. Grandpa opened the gate, got into the truck, and backed away down the lane. In front of him, he saw the cows watching.

Just past the gate leading into the home farm, he wedged the truck in diagonally, blocking the way to the road. He got out and looked down the lane. The cows weren't coming. They were bunched at the open gate.

He cut the twine on one bale of hay and it expanded in the truck bed. He took some of the hay with him and walked toward the cows. He scattered the hay halfway between LBJ and the truck, then got back into the truck and waited. Finally they started to come.

He got out of the truck. He took more of the hay and spread it just inside the gate to the home farm. The cows were coming faster now, like how a broad river speeds up as it goes through a narrow stretch. They filled the lane. They came along, three and four wide, calves tucked into the gaps. Yearlings snorted, pushing the pace. They sped up. Maybe they did know what was going on. They'd probably been without water for twelve hours, maybe twenty. They hadn't had much to eat since yesterday. They were coming home. They were cold. They were hungry.

Grandpa took more hay and walked through the gate to the home farm. This part of the farm had grown up in trees and brush, so there were low branches, brambles, and small fallen trees. He called to the cows. He couldn't see them through the trees. He stopped. He called, but his voice was shut in by the snowy branches. Maybe they'd stopped. Maybe they were confused by the hay in the back of the truck, just out of reach. Maybe they were confused that he'd disappeared. Or maybe they'd come to the truck and kept going. If they were determined, they could squeeze past the truck and get out onto the road.

He stood for a moment in the quiet woods, then went on, northward, and after a couple of minutes he came to a fence. He found another gate there and opened it, pushing it through the snow, and from there he could see across the broad field to the barn and house, about a quarter mile away, and if only the cows would make it this far, they'd know where they were. Maybe asking them to go through the woods was too much. They didn't know these woods. They didn't know what was on the other side.

He waited. He called. He was still carrying some hay. He dropped it. It was no use anymore. Where was the herd? He was about to backtrack when he heard them, a couple of them at least, walking through the woods, snapping branches as they passed, breaking the crust of the snow with their hooves. Then he saw the first one—he recognized her, a big whiteface with a notch in her ear where an ear tag had been torn out when she was a heifer. She came through the trees, looked at him, and kept coming, and went through the gate and headed straight for the barn, not even pausing for the hay on the ground. The others soon followed, dribbling through in twos and threes. The bull came through slowly, lumbering, not even bothering to look at Grandpa. The calves kicked up their heels in the big field. Grandpa stood by and counted.

They all came.

When he got back to the barn, the whole herd was already there, and the dogs were watching the cows. Grandpa gave them their hay. He walked out and chipped through the ice on the pond. He fed the dogs. Ran some fresh water for them. He walked across the southern field, tracing the herd's path, closed all the gates, drove the tractor home, parked it. On the porch he took off his boots, coat, gloves, and cap. Stepped inside. It was after eight. He could tell the furnace had been turned up. He went into the living room. Grandma was in the chair, in her bathrobe, with the heating pad.

"Good morning," she said. She managed a smile. "How long have you been out in that awful cold?"

"I got the cows moved."

"You did? Did Smith help?"

He told her.

"I'll make you a hot breakfast," she said, moving to stand up.

"Cereal will be okay," he said.

But she was up.

Later, he asked her to note in her diary that he'd brought the cows home today. He always had her record these things. She said he should just write it in there himself. She'd never asked that before. In the afternoon—they were taking a break from decorating—he went to the desk in the dining room and got her diary. It was just a small black spiral-bound thing; their insurance man gave them one every year. He opened it up to today. There was no entry. There was no entry yesterday, either. He knew she wrote in this every day. Sometimes she did fill it in a day late, though. So . . . He felt . . . Maybe he would check the journal in a day or two.

On the Monday, December 19, page he wrote: *Brought cows home.*

So, Christmas

The last two days of school before Christmas were snowed out. On the one hand this extended our vacation, and any snow day was a good day—and bright, and too short, and satisfying. But on the other hand, the last week of school before Christmas was generally a fun time—verging on manic—and the hallways smelled of Christmas trees and popcorn that had been popped for both eating and being made into garlands, and everyone got along, and it was common to receive a surprise invitation from another class to come watch a movie with them in their room. (Sit on the floor cross-legged. Eat brownies that had been cut so small they looked like dice.) Missing the last day of school before Christmas also meant being deprived of the in-class and all-school Christmas parties and gift exchanges, and the gratifying white paper sacks filled with salted in-shell peanuts, candy orange slices, chocolate bars, and oranges that the teachers would hand out as we filed out the doors. In addition, the truncated schedule meant we didn't get to say the proper kind of pre-Christmas farewells to our friends: *Well, hope you get a lot of good stuff for Christmas, and call me and tell me what kind of good stuff you get for Christmas.*

Most of the snow fell on Wednesday, the 21st. On Thursday, which would have been the last day of school, we stayed in the farmhouse and made gingerbread cookies—dozens of them—in several different shapes: stars, snowmen, Christmas trees, cows, terriers, candles, hens, and of course gingerbread men. Then we spent the afternoon decorating the cookies with colored icing. Yes, I put too much green food coloring into one cup of icing, but it turned out the be the favorite icing as we decorated the cookies. Hard to beat that kind of green. We kept the wood fire blazing like mad all day because the high temperature was five degrees, and we could feel it dropping as dark fell.

After dinner, Mom and I ventured out. Our long driveway often became impassable after snowfalls and the subsequent drifting, and our remedy was to leave our cars out by the mailbox and walk to them when necessary. So Mom and I dressed for the cold, and I put my black guitar in its black case and carried it over the hill. We got into the hatchback and drove farther down Mount Hope Road—which was smooth and white, as if it had been steamrolled instead of plowed—to the corner where the Bleichs lived. Their tiny white farmhouse was in another county—about fifty feet in—and their farm spread down into the riverbottom. Inside, Darlene gave me my Christmas present. It was a guitar pick holder she had made for me, green with a black "J." It was a bit bigger than a matchbook. I had three picks, all of which exhibited a tendency toward waywardness, so this gift was a welcome thing. We gave her our present—cookies from this afternoon—and then we settled down to lessons. We talked about the weather as I tuned my guitar. Darlene was always one for talking about the weather.

Darlene drilled me in the A minor chord that night, a fine chord if ever there was one, not too hard on the fingertips, and always striking, always evocative. Mom sat by, reading a news magazine. The Bleichs' Christmas tree had big bubble lights on it, which Darlene had told us about last week—how much she loved them, how they reminded her of her childhood. To close out the lesson, we played a few Christmas songs together. I dropped my pick during "O Tannenbaum," but we did a tolerably good job on "What Child Is This?" As far as I could tell, Darlene was the best guitar player alive. Tonight, she gave me two new songs, which, as usual, she had transcribed by ear from the radio, then typed out for me. Often, she put these songs into easier keys, like C or G. This night, she gave me "Ozark Mountain Jubilee" (C) and "I'm Gonna Wake Up in Your Arms Tomorrow" (D), which featured the dreaded B minor chord.

Such was life. As I put my guitar back into its case, Mom and Darlene talked about eggs. Our chickens weren't laying much now that it was winter, and Mom asked how many eggs Darlene could spare. Darlene said she had about five dozen. We bought four dozen—a princely amount—and Mom wrote a check for $12.80, which covered the eggs and the lesson. We drove up the road back toward our farm, and the big hill loomed in front of us, and Mom fretted and downshifted, and we tackled it—Mom leaning forward, as if this helped—making good progress and only spinning a little bit near the top. We left the car at the end of the driveway, locked it, and walked home. The stars were bright, and I was still thinking about guitar chords.

Something about the cold that week made me fall asleep instantly and wake up late. I'd clamber into bed, shivering, wearing knee-high socks under my pajamas, and the TV would be on downstairs because Dad was watching the news, and there were lights on in the girls' room, and I was cold and thought I was getting colder and then I'd fall asleep suddenly, *clunk!*, like I'd been clubbed, then wake up because the sun was on my face and it was time for breakfast.

On Christmas Eve—which in many ways was better than Christmas Day, because the energy of Christmas Eve was accumulative, whereas the energy of Christmas Day dissipated steadily—no one went outside except Dad. He went out after breakfast to find the cows huddled in the barn, of their own volition. They'd been in the barn for over a week. Normally, they came inside only a few times a day, but now it was too cold for them outside. Too windy. Here they had a tank of water—kept from freezing by a small floating heater—and shelter and the warmth of each other. And hay.

To get the hay, as always, Dad climbed into the hayloft, pulled a few bales over to the big opening in the floor, yelled "Look out be*low*!," then heaved them down. The "Look out be*low*!" was both a warning and signal for Teddy, who waited eagerly out of harm's way, then attacked the hay bales with gusto as soon as they landed. It was one of his best skills. Never once did a hay bale put up much of a fight once he had a go at it.

Dad fed the cows and the horses before breakfast, and returned and did the same at dusk. We did not go get the mail, because it was just that cold.

We made pizza dough in the afternoon and put it near the wood stove to rise. After dinner, Mom washed, I dried, and Susan started a batch of lemon cookies, which were her favorite.

We played board games.

Late that night, I watched the weather with Dad. We had put the TV in the study on top of a chest that held old quilts. With the wood fire, this was one of the only rooms that felt warm.

The weather report revealed that the daytime high had been five below, the low tonight could approach twenty below, that records were falling from Denver east, and to top it off, the windchill would be in the negative forties and fifties tonight and in the morning. I'd never heard of such a thing. Throughout the weather report, Dad emitted grunts of pessimistic amazement, as if he'd always known that the weather would turn on us like this, and as if it were permanent.

The weatherman, who was a genuinely pleasant fellow who you wished was your neighbor, sounded apologetic. He clearly felt somewhat responsible for the dangerously cold weather. He pleaded with the viewers not to go out if they didn't have to. But, he said, on a happy note, despite the cold, radar sites had confirmed that Santa *was already on his way.*

"Really?" the news anchorman said. "Because isn't it possible that there are still a few boys and girls who are awake?"

The weatherman explained that Santa started his route in Europe, where it was already the middle of the night. The anchorman accepted this explanation, and to be fair, it made sense, even if it was nonsense, and all for the benefit of any four-year-olds who might be watching.

I got in bed, mind buzzing one moment and then, *clunk!,* I fell asleep.

Sometime in the middle of the night, I woke up. My bed was against the window, and I had a good view. The moon was riding west, casting inky shadows and lighting the snow brightly. It was the kind of scene one might encounter in a picture book, perhaps with the addition of a bushy-tailed fox treading along the edge of the woods, his footprints visible behind him.

The yard, driveway, and fields were covered with snowdrifts, and I could feel the wind seeping in at my window—the enchanting whisper of winter—and I kept myself tucked down into the blankets, but with a clear view out. There were no noises in the house, and no lights on except the Christmas tree lights. I had pleaded for them to be left on overnight, and now they cast patches of color upon the stairwell wall. Outside, far across the countryside, I could see the yard lights of two neighboring farms.

As I lay in bed, looking out at the frigid snowscape, I felt a sense of balance. I was situated neatly between Christmas Eve and Christmas Day. I sensed that if I could remain here forever, in this precise time and place, with this view, with this warmth, with the knowledge that my sisters and parents were all sleeping nearby, I would never be unhappy.

When I woke in the morning, I heard a voice. Dad. Dad was on the phone downstairs. It was getting light out, but the sun wasn't up. I was warm, but I knew if I moved as much as an inch, I would encounter cold air.

I heard Susan say, from the other room, "Jeremy?"

"What?"

"Are you up?"

"Yes."

There was movement in the girls' room. The door opened. Susan was still in her nightshirt. "Are Mom and Dad awake?" she asked.

"I think so."

We listened. We didn't hear anything.

"I heard Dad before," I said.

Susan leaned over the banister, looking down the stairwell.

"Are you guys up?" she called.

There was no answer. We heard water running in the bathroom.

Then we heard Dad's voice, faintly. It sounded like he was on the back porch, on the phone.

"Who's he talking to?" Susan asked.

"Let me sleep," Elizabeth said from the other room, her voice sunken in her pillow. Susan and I smiled.

"No!" I said.

Then I simply exploded out of bed.

There was a fair amount of upstairs–downstairs coordination required. First, we all had to verify that we were all awake. Second, we all had to verify that we were all ready. (For me, being awake meant I was ready. But for Mom and Dad, it seemed more complicated, and we heard them walking around quickly, and even coming into the living room a couple times, and saying things like "Just a minute. . . .") Third, there was the matter of the order in which we children walked down the stairs. This year, when we were ready, I was given the first position, which was a dizzying piece of luck. Then we were told which color wrapping paper Santa had assigned to each of us. And finally we were given permission to descend.

That first step off the top landing, so wonderful, so ripe. The trip down felt like a peculiar kind of floating, and you had to take it one step at a time, carefully, paying attention, because your mind was elsewhere, your mind was crowded, your mind was not interested in simple things like walking down the stairs, and your eyes, too, were hard to control. But you made it, you hit the living room floor—the old yellow pine floorboards—and turned and charged the tree, and there it all was, laid out before you—*everything wrapped in blue is yours*—whereas last night there had been only the modest pile of family presents.

So, Christmas.

When the first rush was over—the Santa presents—there was a natural pause before we moved to the stockings, and that's when they told us we weren't going to Windsor today. Dad had called and talked to Grandpa, and Grandpa had talked to Dad's brother, Kent, who'd also planned to bring his family to Grandma and Grandpa's today, and it was agreed that traveling today wasn't a good idea. It was too cold. We would go tomorrow. And therefore, Mom said, there was no need to hurry—originally, we'd been planning to leave about ten—and so maybe we should wait now, before moving on to the socks, and clean up and have breakfast and then return for the socks and family presents.

This was good. The day was ours. We didn't have to go any-where. We didn't have to go to Grandma and Grandpa's church. We would play with our Christmas presents here and now. It was like a surprise present—to have the day to ourselves, just our family. It was a rare thing for Christmas. It was like another snow day, handed to us suddenly.

Yes, yes, yes! This was all good and wonderful. But. But, we argued, let's go ahead and do socks now, *then* have breakfast, then family presents. Yes, let's do socks now. Let's not wait. Socks, then breakfast.

But Dad had to feed the cows soon.

But we had time to do socks first. We could do it pretty fast. We really could.

So we did.

After that, we all got dressed, and the house was starting to warm up, and we had breakfast after nine. Cinnamon toast, fruit cups, and peppermint tea.

To hit the highlights, Elizabeth got a boom box, Susan got a watch and some boots, and I got an electronic experiment set.

In other words, Santa did occasionally veer from the list I'd supplied and give me a present that was not preapproved. He did, however, put a great deal of thought into these presents, and you had to love him for that, even if the larger (close to overwhelming) feel-ing was one of disappointment. You sometimes fixated on what you didn't get as opposed to what you did. But the electronic experiment set's box advertised sixty working projects, including such prospects as a lie detector and an electronic sleeping aid.

To be more specific, including all the minor Santa presents, sock presents, and Mom and Dad presents, Elizabeth got: an Arabian horse patch, bath cubes, word search books, lipstick, mittens, blouse, and candy.

Susan got: earmuffs, a sparkly pencil, a seam ripper, lipstick, bath cubes, a black cat stuffed animal, three smaller stuffed animals, a turtleneck, a shirt, tights, cookbooks, a little round plastic digital clock with a sticker on the back so you could stick it anywhere, and candy.

I got: a sparkly pencil, cash ($3.00), a calculator, a watch, a small spaceship, a LEGO Cosmic Cruiser, a few action figures, a small action figure cruiser bike, and candy.

The gifts to and from the family were: a strange board game about the Egyptian underworld, a video game cartridge called *Entombed,* which was about an archeologist trapped in the maze under a pyramid, and the official video game cartridge based on the movie *The Raiders of the Lost Ark.* Why all three gifts had Egyptian themes was inexplicable. And the image of Mom pawing through the bargain bin of video game cartridges at the toy store (where she found *Entombed*) was too comical. (It had cost 99¢.)

After noon, then, we hauled the haul upstairs. With warm air rising from the wood stove downstairs and the sunlight streaming into our southern windows, my room and the girls' room were warm. These rooms were the only carpeted rooms in the house, which helped, too. And the girls' room had the chimney running through it, and you could put your hand against it and feel the gentle warmth.

Later, we worked on our video games. It was not usual to play video games with Mom and Dad, but today they joined in. We all five sat there, on the floor, watching the man in the hat move from room to room on the black-and-white TV, making a *pit-pat-pit-pat* noise as he walked. Occasionally he used his whip to some effect. He found a grenade. He tried to figure out how to use it. He blew himself up. We finally turned to the hints section of the rule book, and figured out how to blow a hole in the wall with the grenade, how there was another series of rooms back there, and how if you weren't careful, you'd suddenly step through to someplace new only to find yourself falling through thin air.

The cats—Tracks and her daughter—slept on my bedspread in the sun. The phone did not ring.

"I don't know how to use the parachute," I said, as we progressed further into the game.

We switched to the other game, that bargain-bin fodder, and it was simpler, and happily straightforward. Your little man was at the top of the screen, and from below rose a maze, and you had to navigate your man straight down through this ever-moving maze, avoiding ghosts and dead ends, and if you got stuck or slowed and your man touched the top of the screen—*blip!*—it was the end of you. I'd never heard of this game, but it was good . . . it was great!

To watch Mom playing against Susan, both their little men dashing madly and often illogically about as the maze sped up, and they got so tickled they lost control, and Susan went first—*blip!* Or me playing against Elizabeth, getting to higher and higher levels, the maze speeding up, figuring out the trick about how you could build a wall across your opponent's path, but also soon realizing that this could also accidentally block your own passage. Level seven. *Blip!*

Laughing so hard, sweat rose on your forehead.

The cats, now grooming themselves, now licking each other's faces.

The sun, lowering, lowering.

Everyone in my room. The whole family in my room.

Then later, after dinner, after dark, moving to the girls' room, because it was warmer there, and cozier. We played a board game. Dad put a roll of a new kind of film into his camera, and he took pictures of us without the flash. Would this work? Not using a flash? What would this look like? We huddled.

So, Christmas: Part Two

On the morning of December 26, his forty-fifth birthday, Dad was in motion before dawn. He stoked the fire in the wood stove, dressed, drank some water, gathered the packages—gifts for Grandma, Grandpa, Kent, Lucretia, Brad, Melissa, Aunt Clarice, Aunt Billie, plus the Ruffins—and loaded them into a big cardboard box. This he took outside, tied it onto the Yankee Clipper sled, and started walking, pulling the sled behind him.

He crossed the windswept front hill, the thin steel runners of the sled slicing through the snow. There at the end of the driveway sat our little yellow hatchback.

He opened the car and loaded in the presents. Then he got the mail, which had been sitting in the mailbox since Christmas Eve, and walked home with the empty sled. He made three trips like that, transporting presents and baggage, and then spent a significant amount of time bent over the open hatch of the car, arranging, rearranging, trying to get things to fit. It was one of Dad's talents to pack a car with extraordinary efficiency, but it couldn't be rushed, and by the time he got back to the house and fed the horses and cows and cats and came inside, everyone else was done with breakfast. He ate lukewarm oatmeal with raisins that were as soft as jelly.

We walked out in a row, the snow squeaking beneath our feet. Above us, the hammered-tin ceiling of clouds was bright but relentlessly uniform, and my feet were hot inside my moon boots. When we got to the hatchback, I saw that it was already running. Our station wagon was bigger than this car, but this car had front-wheel drive and a trusty five-speed, and thus we were taking it to Windsor, despite the clown-car stunt required to fit all five of us and our cargo inside. But we did fit, and it was warm in the car, and the engine purred with a reassuring steadiness.

We tried to remember a single time we'd all ridden in the hatch-back together. Not once, we decided, until today.

We traveled west on Highway 50, through a familiar procession of small towns, and I remembered yesterday, Christmas, and won-dered why it had felt so good to be plucked at the last moment from having to spend most of the day at Grandma and Grandpa's. Why dread Grandma and Grandpa's? I hadn't always felt this way. Maybe now that I was older I saw the inconveniences, hoops to be jumped through, and not-home strangenesses more clearly than before. Some things could be singled out as difficult to endure. Like the kisses they gave you in greeting. On the lips! So dreaded. And there was the singing. Oh, heck, all the singing. Each Christmas, our family and Kent's family and Great Aunt Billie and Great Aunt Clarice and Grandma and Grandpa would all gather in Grandma and Grandpa's living room on Christmas night and perform a sort of one-family Christmas music revue—piano solos, piano with voice, voice with voice, voice with pretaped music, and voice solos—and as the youngest I was always the worst, and the days when I had been able to rely on cuteness and a rushed humming of the theme song from a movie were gone. Great Aunt Clarice even tape-recorded these evenings.

Plus, we were outgunned almost to the point of embarrass-ment. Kent was a Baptist minister of music; his wife, Lucretia, his unflappable accompanist on piano; their son, Brad, a nuanced vocal soloist and determined pianist; and their daughter, Melissa, an angelic vocalist. And Grandma had been the church organist for, what?, twenty berzillion years?

I remembered my piano performance last year, a poorly exe-cuted rendition of an easy carol, and how after me Susan had bum-bled her way through "Winter Wonderland." She could play it almost

flawlessly at home, but at Grandma and Grandpa's, with everyone watching, it fell apart. It was hard to watch—Susan brought
down by the pressure. Still, we clapped and grinned and pretended
it was grand. Susan didn't smile. Then it was Grandma's turn to play
something, and she sat down at the piano, opened up a songbook,
and started playing none other than "Winter Wonderland." We
couldn't believe it. Moments after Susan's flawed version, here was
Grandma sight-reading her way through a showy, highly syncopated
and complicated arrangement, playing loudly and perfectly, as if to
wipe Susan's rendition from existence and reestablish what the song
should sound like. We clapped and praised her performance and
didn't make comparisons out loud. My family wondered why she'd
done that, chosen that song at that moment. Why, Grandma? You
usually made us feel good, special.

That, and the way Grandpa would glare at you, as if by simply
being yourself you had committed a crime. He was a tall, imposing
grandpa, with farmer hands as broad as shovels and a certain idea of
what was appropriate behavior for children. For example, he would
long remember the crime of your refusing the zucchini casserole at
dinner. Or the more serious offense of having taken some, but then
leaving the entire portion on your plate, even after he said loudly,
"Aren't you going to eat your casserole?" and you shrugged, wriggled, and he said, "Your grandmother made that for you."

The way Great Aunt Clarice told you not to use the word "weird,"
because when she was young it had meant something very bad.
What had it meant? Why not tell us? "Weird" was a good word, and
we needed it, and to do without it would have been, well, weird.

The fact that of the smattering of presents you got at Grandma
and Grandpa's house, in all likelihood only one or two of them might
be any good, and even then they weren't nearly as good as the good
stuff you got at home. The hierarchy of Christmas presents was a
grim fact of life.

And then there was religion. The church with its bloodred carpet, recessed lights that burned your eyes if you looked up, the slow
parade of words, warnings, hymns you didn't know the tune to. The

standing up and sitting down and standing up and sitting down. Did God really care whether you were standing up or sitting down at this particular moment? All of the Jacksons except us were upstanding church people—what with Kent's profession, and Grandma's organ playing, and Grandpa being a deacon, and Great Aunt Clarice having spent years in service to the Baptist Children's Home. Clarice was, according to Mom, essentially a Baptist nun.

So being not-church-people made Christmas at Grandma and Grandpa's generally slightly uncomfortable and occasionally very uncomfortable. We weren't part of their club, and yet here we were, celebrating their most holy holiday with them. And how about the year Great Aunt Clarice brought the gift exchange at Grandma and Grandpa's to a halt by holding up an unwrapped gift we'd given to her and saying, "Ann and Darrell, how would it make you feel if I refused to accept this gift from you?"

What? What was going on? But Mom had an inkling.

"Then that would be your choice," Mom said.

"Well, not accepting Jesus Christ is like not accepting the greatest gift of all, and it's hurtful and painful to him. To refuse his love and his promise is to dwell in darkness. Christ paid for our sins and only through accepting him as our personal savior are we assured of salvation."

"It's just the blank journal we give you every year," Mom replied, "and if you don't want it, we can buy you something else."

No, she wanted the journal, and she thanked us. She loved her journal.

Perhaps it wasn't fair to compare Christmas at home to Christmas at Grandma and Grandpa's. Besides, there were things there, too, that held a large portion of pleasure and rightness. The way when you wandered into the kitchen in the morning, Grandma was there— there she was, always!—and she would wrap a cinnamon roll in aluminum foil and pop it into the toaster oven and get you situated in a chair and give you a saucer and a knife and the tub of margarine and then unwrap the heated cinnamon roll for you, and the steam coming from it was a vapor of joy, and no matter how good a cook and baker Mom was, Grandma was better, and not afraid to use sugar, and her cinnamon rolls were perfection.

Wrapped in foil! Heated for you! Never, ever a comment about using too much margarine! Not once!

Also, think about that big furnace grate in the floor between the living room and the dining room. That grate, bigger than a doormat. You'd never seen anything like it. It was the only vent in the whole house. You could stand on it, and the hot air surged up—up your pant legs, against the bottom of your chin, through your hair—and you and your sisters and cousins could all squeeze onto the grate at the same time. Barely. That thing.

The barn, with the hayloft and the stalls and the hallway, and the nooks and different ways to climb from below to above and above to below. The smell of hay in your hair—dust, but good dust.

The way Grandma and Grandpa sometimes drove the sedan into the pasture to check on the cows, letting you sit between them in the front seat.

Or how Grandma let you sit beside her when she practiced the organ in the empty church, and how she would let you flip the little switches that were arrayed on the console there, and how sitting beside her there on the red, tufted velvet bench pad you felt as if you were seated with a queen on her throne. Below the organ, tucked neatly alongside each other, Grandma kept a pair of slippers. Whenever she played the organ, she would change out of her heels and into her slippers—because her feet played the big row of pedals down below just like they were another keyboard. After playing, she would change back into her shoes and place the slippers carefully where they dwelled in their tucked-away little corner of the world, day and night, summer and winter, waiting, waiting, waiting for their call to duty. Musical slippers.

Or the big old grain truck, how Grandpa let you ride in the back of it with your sisters and cousins, leaning up against the cab, palms on the red roof, wind in your face, motoring onward toward LBJ . . .

The train, heard passing after sunset, a mile to the south . . .

The landscape, the openness of it. Undulations that mounded

their way east or west, and how when you walked up them you felt like you were ascending to the highest point in the world because the hills at home just weren't this close to the sky . . .

Popsicles in the summertime. Hopping from hay bale to hay bale where they were lined up beside the garden. The exact same Christmas decorations every year, including the painting of the wintry country scene that had glitter on it to make the snow sparkle . . .

Grandma sitting you down at her dressing table and combing your hair with great vigor—the pain, but also the pleasure of it. The little bottles and brushes on the table, the big mirror, the floral, powdery smell there, the way your hair was sleek and large when she was done.

Everything in its place.

Nothing changed.

And Grandpa letting you turn on the CB radio in the car . . . Calling Grandma at home: "Green Giant to Base . . . Green Giant to Base . . ."

"This is Base, over." (Grandma!)

"There's a cowboy here who wants to say hi, over." Passing the handset to you. "Hold this down and talk," he says.

You hold the handset against your mouth. You think. What to say? What? You are five years old.

"This is a cowboy here," you say.

"Let go of the button—the button," Grandpa says.

"—ell, hello, cowboy!" says Grandma.

So: Christmas. Here. There. The countdown, the arrival. Journeys in cars. Frost on the mailbox. Animals depended on us. The oven was still warm inside long after the cookies were done. Cinnamon under your fingernail. Blue bows, silver bows, tan ribbon. Stars through the window. A red candle, dripping.

Uncle Kent, Aunt Lucretia, and Brad and Melissa arrived at Grandma and Grandpa's about an hour after we got there, and as they entered—greetings flying, hugs abutting hugs, exclamations about the weather—the farmhouse went from full to crowded. Kent's family lived in Memphis, and they were called the Memphis Jacksons—we were called the Lohman Jacksons—and their southern accents filled the house and then some.

Kent addressed the Lohman Jackson children: "Now, to be honest, there's one item of bad news we should get out of the way . . ." We listened seriously, but were aware that it was a setup. "We left all the presents in Memphis." He held a solemn look for a moment, then smiled. We laughed.

We kids fetched the presents from Kent and Lucretia's car—dressed not even close to warm enough, but counting on speed and the importance of our mission to make the cold tolerable—and then we took over the living room, put all the presents in place, and were wowed by the amount of real estate covered by wrapped boxes. It was as if a freighter of gifts had run aground on the shoals of the front porch and spilled its cargo across half of the room. A too-short tree only increased the effect. And Brad—who was twenty—had a mustache and a sport coat, and whereas always he had seemed unbelievably old, now I worried that he was unreachable by the likes of me. Was he still funny?

Grandpa appeared in the doorway between the kitchen and the living room, frowning—probably because we were too loud. His hair was looking wild. As quickly as he appeared, he disappeared.

For those of us under the age of sixty, the outfit of the day was: sweaters. The colors represented were: gray, red, kelly green, forest green, teal, cream, navy, burgundy, and gold. The styles in play included: crewneck, V-neck, V-neck vest, cardigan, and scoop neck.

Melissa was Susan's age, and she was allergic to Grandma and Grandpa's house, and she had already started sniffling, and now she sneezed three times in a row. "It's not Christmas without allergies," she said, and we laughed.

Soon Great Aunt Billie and Great Aunt Clarice arrived—they were Grandpa's sisters—and then began a concerted and crowded effort to prepare and serve dinner. Grandma sat at the little kitchen table, slightly hunched. She was in her dressing gown because she

was sick. She directed Lucretia and Mom. She wasn't well enough
to cook.

"Now, Ann, back on the cart there, in the—uh—pitcher, there's
a little wire trivet—see it? Put that on the burner, and with the
burner on low, it'll keep the cheese sauce from scorching."

"Did you want to start a second batch of rolls warming?" Lucretia
asked her.

"Yes, but put the toaster oven as low as it will go, and make sure
they're covered with foil."

"Grandmother," said Brad from the doorway to the dining room,
"I think both of the jams need spoons."

"In the cupboard, in the right-hand drawer," she directed him,
"you'll find a set of four small silver spoons in a white box . . ."

Finally, after one o'clock, we gathered around the maple dining
table—fully extended, with both leaves added—elbow-to-elbow, the
thirteen of us. We carried in a softer chair for Grandma—to make her
more comfortable. I was seated at the corner of the table, and next to
me at the head of the table was Mom, and next to her was Grandma.
Grandpa, at the opposite end, said the blessing.

"Dear Heavenly Father, we thank thee for this joyous day, when
we come together to praise you and your greatness, and thank thee
for all the blessings that we've received this year. We thank thee,
too, for the gift of your son, Jesus Christ, whom we honor this day.
Heavenly Father, we pray that we may prove ourselves worthy of His
love, and, Heavenly Father, we thank thee for the fellowship of our
family, and for the safe travels that brought us together today. And,
Heavenly Father, we thank thee for the bounty that is before us, and
ask you to bless this food and the hands that prepared it, and we ask
you, Father, to help those of us who suffer now, and to give them
strength. We ask this in Jesus' name. Amen."

"Amen," several said. Then we looked up and considered the
table. It was the usual full symphony of Christmas food and decoration. The plates were gold rimmed and depicted small sprigs of holly
and candy canes around the outside edge. Matching the plates were
salad plates and coasters. The drinkware was large red glass tumblers.

On each plate was a napkin printed with a colorful Christmas wreath. The silverware was actual silverware. The food included but was not limited to: turkey, ham, scalloped potatoes, mashed potatoes, green beans, corn, zucchini casserole, cauliflower in cheese sauce, gravy, rolls, cherry-cola gelatin salad, trilayer red-white-and-green gelatin salad, blackberry jam, and margarine. The drink choices were brewed iced tea or water.

"Mother, this looks just *dee*-licious," said Kent.

"I can't take the credit for it," she said. "I just bossed the youngins."

"Well," Kent said, "you and the youngins are a super team, let me tell you."

Food was passed, and there came the sound of serving utensils clicking against plates. Mom plopped some zucchini casserole onto my plate before I could protest.

When all the dishes had made their circuit, we began eating. I poked at my food. I watched Grandma, who was eating very slowly. She seemed all right. Just quiet. Not very hungry. Then, while Elizabeth—at Great Aunt Clarice's prompting—was talking about the colleges she'd applied to, Grandma hunched down, just slightly, and closed her eyes and stayed like that for a few moments. Then she straightened back up.

"Are you all right, Mother?" Kent asked.

"I am." She aimed her fork for her plate.

Nobody said anything. We chewed and swallowed, drank iced tea, wiped our mouths, and spread margarine on rolls.

"I have to say," Brad finally said, "that looking at this table, it's like I'm in some spectacular dream where delicious food is just floating around me and I can reach out and eat whatever I want."

We laughed.

"You mean to tell us," Great Aunt Billie said, "that you don't eat like this at college?"

"Hm," Brad said, mock-considering, "not quite."

"I've often wondered how an apartment full of boys manages with cooking," Aunt Clarice said.

"Ha!" Grandpa laughed.

"Let me put it this way," Brad said. "Without instant rice, we would starve." We laughed. "That reminds me. Earlier in the semester, Grandmother mailed me a nice box of cookies, and I ate a few the day I got them, then went to the library that night to study. And I made the mistake of leaving the cookies out in plain sight, and when I came back the cookies were gone, and I'm pretty sure someone had licked up the crumbs, too."

We laughed. Brad.

As we laughed, Grandma smiled, but then she lowered her head. Closed her eyes. And groaned. We heard. In her dressing gown. Her hair not neat.

On my plate, cold mashed potatoes.

I had seen Grandma walk from the kitchen to the dining room leaning on Dad. I had rarely, in my life, seen her in her dressing gown. Now here she was eating Christmas dinner in it, and I didn't know what it meant. Yes, we'd been warned that Grandma had been feeling unwell, but . . . too sick to dress? She'd been to my Christmas music program just ten days ago and had seemed fine.

She remained hunched down in her chair, and soon Kent and Mom ushered her away from the table so that she could sit in a soft chair in the living room. She didn't protest. She did not urge us to go ahead with dinner. She didn't say she didn't want to be a bother. This was not like her. She was in pain.

We did continue eating. What else could we do?

Brad jumped into the middle of things in the kitchen. "I'll wash," he said. And the counter became heaped with dirty dishes, and an assembly line formed around him—sorting dishes, storing leftovers, drying dishes, putting dishes away. A small collection of dishes was left on the kitchen table. These were items no one knew where to store.

After lunch, Susan was sick, and sat on the toilet for a long time, and Mom went in to check on her and Susan said, "I didn't know that Grandma was so sick."

"I know," Mom said. "We didn't either."

"What's wrong with her? She couldn't eat."

"She has pain in her shoulders and neck. And she's had stomach problems that keep her from eating well."

"She couldn't get dressed."

"Well, sometimes when you're sick, think about how you stay in your pajamas all day."

"But she's Grandma."

Later, Melissa threw up.

The house was like a minefield of candy. It always was at Christmas, and we Lohman Jacksons were not acclimated to such sweetness and richness and we had a tendency to gorge ourselves. Clarice fretted at us and said, "You're going to make yourselves sick, eating candy after a big meal," and Grandpa shook his head in disappointment. But that just made us eat more candy.

Suddenly, we realized that we kids were alone with Grandma in the living room. All the other adults were busy elsewhere. Brad was standing behind Grandma's chair, rubbing her shoulders.

"Grandma, do you want some candy?" Elizabeth asked, holding the dish in her direction. It was an inadequate gesture, but it was what we could do.

"I best not," she said. "Spoil supper." She smiled.

Three presents and two cards sat on the television console. They were for Dad's birthday.

Billie and Clarice drove to Clarice's apartment in Windsor after dark—after the gift exchange and late supper of sandwiches. There would be no all-family music revue this year.

The rest of us, as usual, stayed at the farmhouse. The bedrooms upstairs were unheated, but Mom and Lucretia had remembered to turn on the electric blankets early. Downstairs, Susan and Melissa slept in the twin beds in the back bedroom—also unheated except for a little space heater that would intermittently click on, glow like the father of all toasters, then click off. Elizabeth took the couch in the living room, and Brad and I camped on the floor. Grandma and Grandpa's bedroom was just off the living room, through a big open doorway.

I lay in my sleeping bag on the floor, waiting for the house to get quiet as the long saga of bedtime—eleven people and one bathroom—played out. Grandma was already in bed, in the dim bedroom that I could see into. From the bedroom came the sound of Grandpa blowing his nose like a trumpet.

Then Grandpa emerged. He turned down the thermostat. Unplugged the Christmas tree lights. He barely navigated around me, lying there midfloor.

Somebody dropped something on the floor upstairs. A shoe? Melissa sneezed in the distance.

Looking over at Elizabeth, lying on her side on the couch, I saw that her eyes were open. She smiled a very small smile for me.

Brad lay between us, on his back, as still as a mummy.

"Grandpa," Brad said, "is there anything I can help you with?"

Grandpa was shuffling through our room again, muttering, seeming put upon. "Eh?"

"Is there anything I can do?" Brad asked.

"No."

"Goodnight, Grandpa."

"'Night."

I closed my eyes. I thought back to the early part of the evening— just before supper—when we'd gathered in here and watched a slide-show of Kent and Lucretia's recent trip to China with Kent's choir. I had watched the slides, but I had also watched Grandma in the dimness of the room—watched her watching the slides—and there was something eerie about observing her in the light reflected from a slideshow. It was a pale light, somewhat watery, and made her look unreal, like Grandma but also not-Grandma. It had made me uneasy, the sensation that she wasn't fully there, but I could not stop looking.

On the morning of the 27th, people walked around my sleeping form for quite some time before I sat up. It was another dim morning. Brad was still asleep, but Elizabeth was sitting up reading in her nightclothes. The door to the bathroom was closed. The Christmas tree lights were still off.

I heard Kent call up the stairs. "Darrell?"

When Kent, Dad, and Grandpa were gathered in the kitchen, Kent said, "I don't think Lucretia and I quite realized the severity of Mother's situation. We've got to do something. She shouldn't be in pain like this."

"We can call the doctor, see if he can see her today," Grandpa suggested.

"He's been treating her for months and she's only gotten worse," Kent said. "What she's going through right now doesn't seem like the kind of thing she should have to endure. Darrell?"

Dad, sitting at the table, nodded. "I agree. Ann and I are surprised by how much worse she is than when we saw her just a couple weeks ago."

"What do you mean?" Grandpa asked. "Take her to . . . to the hospital?"

"Yes," Kent said.

"We could wait till tomorrow," Grandpa said, "till your families are gone, so we don't disrupt . . . Christmas."

"We could ask her," Dad offered. "Does she want to go now or tomorrow?"

They asked. She said now, and the shape of the day re-formed itself.

Mom helped her get dressed. Grandma was so stiff and sore she couldn't dress herself, and with Grandma sitting at the edge of the bed and Mom pulling a blouse down over her head, Mom could smell her. She had a smell because she hadn't been able to bathe herself in days. This lapse of hygiene was completely uncharacteristic of Grandma, and it, as much as anything, was a sign to Mom that this illness was more than anyone had guessed.

"I'll tell you, Ann," Grandma said, "I'm glad the weather delayed you all. Because I had a plain horrible day on Christmas . . . felt just awful . . . and I don't think I could have gotten things ready. I just couldn't have done it. So it worked out well, in that respect."

"We can thank the weather for that, then," Mom said.

They picked out a pair of shoes.

Such Hope

There was a warm spell after Christmas.

One afternoon, Elizabeth had basketball practice and Mom was in Kansas City, so Susan and I rode the school bus home. I rested my forehead on the window and felt the jitterings of the gravel road. The bus was mostly empty, and we rumbled our way up the steepest hill of Mount Hope Road, came over the top, then whooshed down the hill and coasted up the next one toward our driveway. Because we rode the bus irregularly, we rose from our seats and stood in the aisle to ensure that the driver saw us and remembered to stop.

The bus deposited Susan and me at the end of the driveway and despite the wind from the southwest it was warm enough that we took off our coats for the walk over the hill. December's snow had melted.

At home, we unlocked the back door and Teddy made a sneaky move and tried to bolt inside. We squealed and blocked him with our legs. He rooted among our shins—strong-snouted pup—and Susan shouted for him to stop, but he didn't, and then she ordered him to get on his rock, and he did. His rock was a piece of limestone about the size of a milk crate. It sat near the stoop.

Susan went inside. I put my bookbag down. Teddy looked at me. "I'm staying out here," I said to him. His valiant attempt to enter the house had inspired me toward outdoor adventure.

I was just one boy, I knew, but there were things a boy could do, I felt, that were significant.

It was like spring, temperature-wise, but there was no greenness, only muck and druck and already-low sun. Tracks, the black cat, had appeared, attracted by the possibility of getting into the house. I walked into the shed and looked for the other cat, but she wasn't there, so I went back outside and walked to the catalpa tree. I climbed up the trunk and hung from the second-lowest branch. I had the full attention of the cat and the dog and I let go with one hand and said, "I can still hold on," even though I could feel the inadequacy of my grip. A few seconds later I fell, and my feet splatted onto the muddy lawn. The cat bolted away. I looked at my palm, and there was a little blood. It started to hurt, so I shook it, but that made it worse. I went inside and washed my hands in the bathroom. Sting it did, and pinken the soap suds.

I was just one boy. A boy whose grandmother was sick, whose dog was a mud-crusted ragamuffin, whose nightmares featured flooded rivers, and whose hand was bleeding in innumerable places at once, like a crop of roses blooming in fast-forward profusion.

I hoped to someday have a stronger hand. To hold on to a branch.

Mom drove behind Grandpa's Pontiac out of the heart of Kansas City, into Raytown, down the Blue Parkway, then through Lee's Summit on Highway 50, and on east from there. As an immense sunset loomed behind them, they turned on their headlights. The traffic thinned. Mom noticed the snow was gone from the fields.

They stopped in Warrensburg at a buffet.

"If she could just eat better," Grandpa said, "she could get stronger. She could come home."

He'd just returned from his third trip to the buffet, and Mom wondered if maybe he was eating for her—for Grandma—or if this was simply the appetite of a man without someone to cook for him for the first time in his life. Her own plate was clean. She had looked at the desserts but been disinclined.

In the early afternoon, Grandpa and Mom had left the hospital and driven to an office complex nearby. They walked across the breezy parking lot, and once they checked in were taken immediately into the specialist's private office. He talked about Grandma's case being a "difficult presentation." He used words that weren't specific, but which accumulated in such a way to indicate the seriousness of Grandma's situation. A team would be assembled. More tests. Best options.

Mom had suspected at the time that Grandpa hadn't heard the gravity of the doctor's news. Or he'd heard it, but not let it into himself. Now, hours later, here he was saying that if Grandma could just eat better, she would be okay. He was a farmer. Food was life. Food was medicine.

Mom pushed her plate to the side. Here was her husband's father, whom she had known for twenty-five years, whom she had spent more time with as an adult than she had with her own father. She remembered the moment just after her wedding ceremony when Grandpa had bent to kiss her and she'd been confused and moved her face the wrong direction and he'd ended up kissing her forehead.

"Belford," she said now, "food isn't going to heal Mildred. She's not sick from hunger. She's sick because of the disease, and she's not eating well because part of the disease is in her stomach. What the doctor was saying today is that Mildred is extremely sick, and that we should be prepared for dire news. What we can do is be with Mildred. We can work with the doctors. We can pray." She was surprised to hear herself say this last thing, but she realized she meant it.

He heard it that time. He let it in. Mom could tell. He stopped eating. He drank his water, emptied it. The ice cubes rattled in the crimson tumbler.

They parted there. Mom drove home to her children and husband. Grandpa drove on to his own house. He arrived home, turned on the lights in the kitchen. The calendar hung on the wall, last year's calendar. December.

He turned on the lights in the living room. There stood the Christmas tree. There was the garland above the doorway. It wasn't eight o'clock yet. He went to the kitchen and washed the smattering of dishes. Then he went upstairs, got the empty boxes, brought them down. He took the ornaments off the tree. He took the Christmas lights off. He didn't know how these things were supposed to be packed, so he just sort of jumbled them into boxes. There were still a few presents—opened, resting in their boxes—under the tree. Most of these were hers. He moved them to the piano bench.

He took the tree out the front door and rolled it off the end of the porch.

Back inside, there was more to deal with. There were Christmas candles, straw wreaths, a homemade quilted wall-hanging that had pockets to hold Christmas cards. In it were dozens of cards. Above the doorway to the bedroom hung a garland of tinsel hoops—red, green, silver. On the mirror above the television: a bell that lit up red and green, from which hung frosted pine cones on strands of red ribbon. On the television: twelve silver bells in a row. Above the stereo cabinet: some sort of cornucopia. Hanging on the wall: a sort of Christmas caterpillar made out of felt fabric with a smiling face and letters spelling "NOEL" on the segments of its body. Another bell. A string of paper letters spelling "Merry Christmas." And more.

In the kitchen window, above the sink, a small sun-catcher clung to the glass with a suction cup. The sun-catcher was two eighth notes joined by a bar. He took it off the window, then looked at it in his palm. The glass body of the first note was orange, the glass of the bar was green, and the second note was pale yellow—like a wet piece of lemon candy. The lead wire that outlined and connected the bits of glass was black. He held the thing, wondering if it was a Christmas decoration. He wasn't sure. It was a sun-catcher. A couple of notes. Somebody had given it to Grandma . . . a few years ago. Now he remembered: it wasn't a Christmas decoration. It was hers. It hung here year-round. He reattached it to the window and continued his work. Putting it all away.

Because the last two days of school before Christmas had been snowed out, we had our school Christmas parties during the first week of January. Delayed, not forgotten. The cinder-block hallway that connected the cafeteria to the school was always cold, a passage to be hurried through. We played bingo. ("B4. B4.") Ate ice cream bars. Drank grape juice. Later that day, at recess, I did not pick Kathy

Smith for my kickball team. She stood there expecting me to pick her, but I didn't call her name, and she refused to play for the other team, and walked away and cried. So that was something I did.

It was indoor kickball.

A treble clef. A bass clef.

A bottle of glitter, spilled.

The warm weather escalated into the weekend. All traces of snow vanished except for patches of white in the deep woods, like exposed bits of a glimmering bedrock.

Saturday I helped Elizabeth lead the horses up the driveway to the south pasture. We let the horses in there, then took off their halters. Almost immediately they came to life. It was nearly sixty degrees, and the two Arabians galloped away from us along the ridgeline. To watch them run was like being involved in something entirely new and exceptional, even though we'd seen it many times. Their barn pasture was too small for much sprinting, but here they could stretch out, and their tails streamed behind them, and they left the ridge and ran down the hill, along the fenceline, and then cut into the wooded draw. For some moments we couldn't see them, but we imagined their progress—visualized it—and anticipated their reappearance, and suddenly there they were, out of the trees, striving, heading back uphill toward us. There was the sound of their hooves, too, and Elizabeth and I hopped to the other side of the fence, not because we were scared but because we were mindful of the power at hand and had no wish to interfere or distract.

The horses wheeled in front of us, then sprinted away again, and Elizabeth said—in a low voice, speaking for them—"We are horses. So we run."

Once

He had known Kansas City.

In 1942, Belford went there and stayed with Mildred's brother, Emmett, and Emmett's wife. Emmett worked in a flour mill. Belford was hired at a munitions factory east of the city. Soon he bought a small house—408 North Wheeling—and Mildred and the boys came. Darrell was three and a half, Kent just a tot.

The Lake City Arsenal was built on good farmland out on Highway 24. To enter, you had to show your pass and open your lunch bucket for inspection. Inside Building #2, Belford was the tool setter for the final inspection of .30-06 cartridges, calibrating machines to tolerances of one-thousandth of an inch to measure the depth of the primer seating, the case dimensions, the weight of the powder, and more. At lunch, he sat at the end of the loading platform and could see the traffic on the highway and smell the cornfields that grew right up to the fence. Inside the arsenal, the smells were machine oil and molten lead.

In the autumn, a letter came from his draft board asking him to report. His classification was 1-A. He figured he would be in the service in a matter of weeks, so he made plans to sell the house and for Mildred and the boys to live with her parents near Bryson. Then, quickly, a second letter came stating that he would not need to report. There was no explanation.

Their neighborhood was filled with people like them, families from small towns and farms, there for work. The Rohrs, the Moores, the Kimmises, and the Heslops. A street of one-story houses. When

Belford worked the third shift, he had to sleep during the afternoon, but found it nearly impossible with all of the kids running in the street, shouting, playing ball. He would put a pillow over his head, then wake up sweating.

At the factory, when people worked carefully and the machines were maintained, all went well. After a year, he moved to another building at the arsenal and began inspecting small carbine cartridges, which were easier to make than the .30-06 because of their straight casing. Later he monitored .50-caliber machine-gun cartridges, which were so big they resembled little pop bottles. The final steps in inspection for all rounds included using a headspace gauge to ensure proper chambering. The cartridges were also weighed. If they were too light it meant they didn't have enough powder in them, and they were sent to the bullet puller to be scrapped.

When the war ended, the job ended. He was hired as an electrician's assistant for an elevator company, hauling electric motors and huge coils of cable—looped over his shoulders—up the dim stairwells of the big buildings downtown. The wind was always more powerful on the rooftops than at street level, and rain made the tarred roofs slick. He wouldn't go out drinking with his bosses, so they didn't like him, and fired him.

At Benson Manufacturing, near the Sears store, he was a metal polisher. One day he was asked to man a machine that he hadn't been trained to use. There was a big polishing wheel situated diagonally behind a charger gate, but the gate kept jamming, and as he tried to force the bar stock through, his right hand slipped and was pulled under the big wheel. They took him to Lutheran Hospital, where his ring finger and pinky were amputated, and his middle and index fingers were set in a splint. Even after twelve weeks, he couldn't flex the remaining fingers well, so Benson switched him over to welding bungholes in aluminum barrels. They let him go in '47.

On his first night as a machinist helper for the Milwaukee–Kansas City Southern Railway, a coal-burning engine came huffing into the roundhouse with a bad connection, spewing coal smoke. He coughed so bad he thought he would die, but after that the smoke never bothered him, though he hated the taste and smell of it. Most of the engines were diesel, anyway. He usually worked the midnight shift, and his foreman told him that if there was nothing to do, he should just make himself scarce. He'd climb into a parked engine and sleep. When an engine approached, the vibration would wake him up. At the end of the shift, the sun would rise, gleaming on the rails all across the wide yard, and he would arrive home to find Mildred awake. For a week he tried to drink coffee to keep awake until the boys were up, but it didn't work, and he never drank coffee after that. To him, it tasted like coal smoke.

Kent was quieter than Darrell, and didn't even like to leave the house for school. But when Kent was seven, he was invited to a birthday party across the street, and when he didn't come back after a couple of hours, Mildred went to fetch him and saw that he was playing at the end of the street with several boys. He came home at dark, but only after Darrell went and got him. After that, it was as if the little house couldn't hold the boy. Some switch had been thrown in him, and he was always out, always about, coming home with grass stains on the ankles of his socks, with sand in his hair, with a bump on his forehead that he claimed he didn't remember receiving. It wasn't just the house that couldn't hold him, but the street, the neighborhood. He went to a junkyard down in the riverbottom, and brought back a hubcap that he hid in the backyard. Mildred found it, and Belford threw it out. He snuck into a warehouse several blocks away, on Gladstone, and came home bragging about it.

"A little roaming is fine," Mildred told Belford late that night, "but roaming with no sense of boundaries is different. Crossing busy streets. Poking around junkyards."

"He's a smart boy," Belford said. He was eating. He would be leaving for the rail yard soon.

"But cleverness courts trouble," she said.

One blustery March day, Kent didn't come home with Darrell from school. It had been spitting rain since noon, and Darrell sat listening to the radio and drawing at the kitchen table. After five,

Mildred asked him to go look for his little brother. It was a task he had become accustomed to. He put on his coat and hat and walked down the street looking for kids. Everyone was inside. He knocked on a few doors and asked after Kent, but no one had seen him.

He walked into the woods back behind the neighborhood, and went through them along the pathway the boys used, and came to the old Indian mound. There was no one there. The mound stood on a bluff and had a sweeping view of the city to the south and west, the riverbottoms to the north. The clouds moved quickly over the city. He went home empty-handed.

When Kent finally came in, Belford was putting on his coat, and Mildred was calling around to the mothers of the neighborhood. The boy was soaked to the skin—even though the rain was intermittent—and he told them that he and Gary Heslop had gone all the way to the lot behind the Montgomery Ward to watch the circus unload. It was the farthest he'd ever gone.

"You're making your mother sick with worry," Belford told the boy. "Is that what you want?"

"No," he said.

"But you're doing it," Belford said. "Making her sick."

"I'm sorry, Mother," he said. Then, by way of explanation, "It was the circus."

"Never mind it for now," Mildred said. "Let's get you dry."

There was the smell of biscuits being kept warm in the oven, and the sound of the rain on the windowpanes, and a car, nearby, trying to start.

Kent sat in the back of a DC-9, three thousand feet above Kansas City. On approach to the airport, the jet dropped below the clouds and tilted its wing toward the ground. The Missouri River revealed itself immediately below Kent, and beyond it stood the old bluffs and empty January woods.

Grandpa was there to pick him up, and as they drove south into the city, Kent asked about Grandma—how she was feeling about tomorrow's operation, and what the doctors were saying. He asked again about the diagnosis—the reason for the neck surgery—because though he had heard it on the telephone, he couldn't remember it exactly. He knew what it meant, more or less, and understood that there was a risk of paralysis if it went untreated, as well as the continued escalation of her discomfort. He also understood that there was an exploratory aspect to the procedure. But he wanted to know the words, too, because they were part of it.

Grandpa didn't know the exact words.

Dad was in the room with Grandma when they arrived. It was the four of them—Grandma, Grandpa, Dad, and Kent—in a hospital room. The family. When was the last time it had been just the four of them together?

A tapping of raindrops on the window.

"Were the roads wet?" Grandma asked.

"Not when we were out," Kent replied.

"Hard to tell what's going on outside from here," she said.

"Nothing good goes on outside in January," Grandpa ruled.

"I tell you, Mother," Kent said, sitting at the foot of her bed, "when we were coming in for a landing, we skimmed right over the old neighborhood, right over North Wheeling Avenue. Like I could have reached down and touched it."

Later, Kent and Dad spoke with one of the doctors in the hallway, and they got these words: "distraction of the C6 vertebral body with metastatic disease."

But these words didn't help. Because where did they go? What did they say?

The doctor was still talking. "But if I had to, I'd guess it's not likely to be well defined. And then there's the issue of where's the source, you know? We've got something here, no doubt about that, but this is probably just the surface, part of the disease that has come up from somewhere else. Nine chances out of ten, there's something older. And from what I can tell, it's more like ten chances out of ten."

Belford got two traffic tickets during the years in Kansas City. One was for running a stop sign. It was on his regular route to the Lake

City Arsenal, so he knew the road well, but the stop sign was brand new and surprised him. That's why he cruised through it. The explanation didn't get him out of a ticket, though. Three weeks later, the sign was taken down.

The other ticket was for a burned-out taillight. Actually, it was just a few days after Kent wandered down to spy on the circus. The thing was, he'd just gotten the light fixed, and here it was, out again, inexplicably. He walked to the back of his car with the policeman and explained the situation, but the cop was already writing up the citation. Belford knocked the fender with the side of his fist, and the light came on—and stayed on—but he still got a ticket. He stood there on the shoulder of the highway, even as the cop pulled away, and he knocked the fender a few more times. The taillight stayed on. He drove home, left the lights on, got out, knocked the fender again. The light remained steady. He was too mad to sleep that night. The city was no good. Cops that didn't listen to reason. Stop signs that were just traps.

That, and the grunt-work jobs. Being told what to do. Labor. His first job out of high school had been digging ditches to lay gas lines in Windsor, then years in the shoe factory and the coal mines, and now here he was, eighteen years later, still doing grunt work for someone else. Sweating, stinking, backaches, lost fingers, late shifts, diesel fumes, union dues, bar-stool bosses, no way up. An executive he'd befriended at Sears, Roebuck told him he might get a job at the company, but without a college degree he'd never advance.

And Kent, wandering.

He and Mildred talked. Spring was a time to make new plans.

On April 23, 1948, Ed Shipp from Windsor, whose trucking business's motto was "Ship by Shipp," brought a load of cattle to the Kansas City stockyards. He cleaned out the truck real good, then went to 408 North Wheeling, loaded up Belford and Mildred's household, and moved them to the farm.

Distance

Me. My room. My carpet. Lolling on my stomach. Perusing the booklet that came with my surprise Christmas present—the electronic experiment set. Many of the experiments had names that evoked profound malaise. *Number 31: Continuity Tester. Number 26: Signal Injector.*

I flipped back to *Experiment Number 1*. Nine blocks. I snapped them into the grid as depicted. Easy. The tiny light bulb in the green plastic circuit block lit up. But it was not a bright bulb. It was dim to the point of pointlessness.

Downstairs, the sound of the oven door thumping shut.

Experiment Number 2: Direction of Current and Rectification. What? I thought not. I flipped ahead. I picked out an experiment that showed how to build a radio.

As I was working, Elizabeth came up the stairs and went into the girls' room. She closed the door. Just after that the phone rang, and I heard Mom answer in the kitchen. I listened. The house was small and my room positioned such that I could hear whatever was spoken anywhere, as long as it wasn't behind a closed door.

I quickly determined that it was Dad on the phone, and so I thought of him, and Grandma, and Kansas City, and surgery, for about the fiftieth time today. I pictured an operating room again, a bright light over the table—which I imagined as similar to the light a dentist used—and then I tried again to think about what it meant to be put under anesthesia, of being unconscious but safe, unfeeling but alive. I remembered my classmate Craig, who'd had an appendectomy a few years ago and under anesthesia had experienced the sensation of running so fast he started to fly. Then I tried to think of what sleep felt like, and this was a particular problem that I had encountered for years. Because no matter how much I bent my mind toward the purpose of recording and cataloging the experience of sleep, once I fell asleep I lost all ability to do any such things, and therefore woke up knowing nothing new. I remembered being asleep, sort of, but I didn't really remember what it was like. So all this was the best I could do by way of imagining Grandma's surgery today, and I knew it was an inadequate imagining.

Mom's voice betrayed no surprise or particular emotion, and so I did not fear for Grandma.

Dinner was lasagna, and it was hot, hot, hot, so I spread it out across my plate—disassembling the layers—so it would cool. While we ate, Mom told us that Grandma was okay, that the diseased bone that had been hurting Grandma's neck was now gone. We knew it didn't mean she was healed totally. Just healed partially.

Elizabeth left in the pickup. Susan, Mom, and I followed about twenty minutes later in the station wagon. We drove to Russellville in the dark and parked outside the school where the teachers usually parked, paid our admission (25¢ plus 25¢ plus $1.00), and went inside. The biggish, squarish lobby was full of adults and kids, and we went through it and into the gymnasium. Mom saw her friend Anne and went up the bleachers to sit by her, Susan walked across to where the high school students sat, and I stood there in the doorway because it was the best place to think about my next move. While I stood there, a cheer went up at the far end of the gym, and the opponent's varsity girls team charged out of their locker room and onto the golden wood of the court. "Boo!" I said, and a high school guy—a classmate of Elizabeth's—looked down at me and said, "Right on," and I felt proud. Our team emerged a moment later with Elizabeth at the back, which I figured was a place of honor. They started warming up in front of me, doing lay-ups, and I looked up at the guy who'd just spoken to me and said,

"Oh, this is going to be no contest!" But the guy didn't hear me that time.

Mom gave me two quarters and a dime and I went to the concessions stand. The concessions were housed in the kindergarten room, which had sliding panels in the wall that could be opened onto the lobby, and I stood at one end of the counter for a good ten minutes, weighing my options. I narrowed it down to: candy bar, soda, chips, or popcorn.

I left. I needed more time. I went down the hallway and talked to a couple of kids who were a year younger than I was. In the background were the cheers of the ball game. These kids and I got into a discussion about how far a mile was. I knew exactly how far a mile was. It was six laps around the school's track. The kids didn't believe me and wouldn't hear reason, and then they raised their real question, which was whether a person could run a mile in one minute. One kid's dad had said something about someone running a mile a minute. Pretty soon, we were arguing about whether the fastest horse in the world could beat the fastest dog in the world. The argument was going nowhere so I walked away. I returned to the concessions stand, handed over my money for a bag of popcorn and then I went and stood in the doorway to the gym again, because food was not allowed inside.

It was the start of the fourth quarter and Russellville was down twenty points and they looked worn out. I watched, tried to figure out what was happening. The opponent was Belle, and they were making Russellville run a lot. They also had a center who, although she wasn't taller than Elizabeth, was about three times wider, and yet remarkably quick, and she was blocking Elizabeth out, and smothering the rebounds.

During a time-out, I watched our team huddled around the coach, and I could see that Elizabeth was mad, and saying something to the coach, and then addressing her teammates. One of her teammates stood with her arms crossed, ignoring Elizabeth.

Then here came Wayne walking down the baseline toward me.

"Wayne-o!" I said.

"Hey, bud," he said.

"Why are they losing?"

"Because when they do pass the ball to Elizabeth, she's getting battered by that truck."

I nodded. That truck. She was getting battered by that truck.

He went into the lobby. Probably getting some popcorn, I thought.

The ball was back in play, and the Russellville parents' section was pretty subdued, but the mother of one of the players was chattering incessantly, giving cheerful advice that everyone in the gym could hear. Like "Let's hustle on defense, girls!" and "Keep your eyes on the ball!"

I watched a couple of minutes of play and could clearly see that Russellville wasn't getting its offense set up very well, but then on one possession, Catherine Gue put up a screen for Elizabeth and Elizabeth slid under the basket and came out toward the sideline— near me—and was wide open. Lo and behold, Carrie passed the ball to her, but too late, the barbarians were upon her, and she was double-teamed and stuck near the corner, just feet from me, and she was mad and trying to find a way to pass the ball out of that mess, and the chattering mother, the one who'd been coaching from the stands, said, loud and clear, "Bounce pass, honey!" as if it were the obvious answer, and Elizabeth stopped looking around for a pass and held the ball and looked right up into the stands at this woman and yelled, "Shut up!"

We got home pretty late. I finished the transistor radio on my electronic experiment set, then double-checked everything, because I feared that even the slightest blunder had the potential of turning a simple experiment into a ball of fire.

I plugged in the earphone and turned the set on. I fit the earphone into my ear and fiddled with the volume knob, and yes, there was static. It was working. I turned the tuning knob, and finally I

found a station. I had done it, I had made a radio—but the station
I'd found was a country station, so I twiddled the tuning knob again
and found another country station, and the sound was bad, bad, bad,
and staticky, and then I figured it out, I realized what this was. This
was an AM radio. So, in other words, useless.

In the morning, Elizabeth asked if she could skip the first hour of
school, and Mom said that was fine. Mom left with Susan and me, and
Elizabeth dragged herself back upstairs to bed. Usually, basketball
didn't make her feel like this—sore and beat down. But Belle had
run them into the ground. Belle had fast plays, fast passing, and that
behemoth who'd guarded Elizabeth would just brush Elizabeth out
of the way with her hip. Elizabeth's own hips were bruised.

Elizabeth got back into bed and closed her eyes, but her mind
went in circles: thinking about the game, how horribly she had
played—five points!—and how horribly the team had played, how
she had yelled at her teammate's mother, how basketball would be
even harder in college, the remaining college applications, how she
didn't want to leave Wayne for college, how track would be harder in
college, too, how track started in less than two months, how graduation was just four months away, how Mom and Dad had told her—not
Susan or me—how serious Grandma's illness was, which made her
wonder how sick Grandma must feel, which made her remember how
bad her own body felt now, which reminded her of the game again.

She heard Mom come home in the car, and then come into the
house, and ten minutes later it was time to get up and get dressed.
Dad was coming home from Kansas City today and needed the
pickup truck to go get cattle feed, so Mom would give Elizabeth a
ride to school.

Outside, she was surprised by how cold it was. It had been mild
since New Year's, but this morning was icy—winter was back. The
red station wagon was still slightly warm inside from taking Susan
and me to school, and Mom asked some questions about the game as
they drove out the driveway and up Mount Hope Road, but Elizabeth
wasn't in a mood to talk about it.

From the top of Mount Hope Road, it was about four miles into Russellville, and Elizabeth felt discombobulated—from the way her body felt, and the way that it was slightly weird to be going to school an hour late, and from feeling generally crowded and unsettled. And hungry. She hadn't eaten.

The parking lot in front of the school was quiet and calm, and Mom handed her a note to excuse her tardiness, and Elizabeth thanked Mom for making two trips to school this morning, and then Elizabeth got out of the car and there, on the car's rooftop, scrunched up at the back of the luggage rack, was a ball of black fur.

It made a tiny sound.

"Tracks?!" Elizabeth yelped.

"What?" Mom asked, leaning toward the open door.

"It's . . . ," Elizabeth said. She reached for the cat, lifted her. She said, "Tracks was on the roof."

Deep

Because of the darkness, and the stillness, and the feeling of being perfectly situated within a sleeve of warmth, it took me a while to realize I was awake. I had come to the surface somehow, out of a deep sleep, and I was lying on my side looking across my room. I saw that Mom was sitting in the big reading chair facing the eastern window of my room. This did not surprise me. I didn't put any thought into the situation. She was Mom. She was sitting in my room. Then, as sleep receded, my mind quickened just enough to put the situation into context. She was here because my room contained the one window in the house with a clear view across the valley to the top of Mount Hope Road. She was watching for Elizabeth to come home. Watching for the wide-set headlights of the pickup truck coming down the road.

I knew that on nights when Elizabeth was out, Mom set her alarm for one a.m. If Elizabeth returned before then, it was Elizabeth's duty to go into the dark study, tell Mom and Dad she was home, and turn off the alarm clock. If the alarm went off, it meant Elizabeth had broken curfew, and Mom would get up and wait. On occasion I did hear the pickup truck coming home in the middle of the night. But not usually. On occasion I did hear Elizabeth in the study—the entire house dark—saying "I'm home," and then the mumble as Mom or Dad acknowledged it and the footsteps of Elizabeth creeping up the stairs. Sometimes I'd hear when Mom would confront Elizabeth for coming in late.

Tonight, I applied no effort to the moment—didn't try to stay awake, didn't try to return to sleep. But return to sleep I did, and it must have come relatively quickly, and been relatively deep.

Later that night, Elizabeth wrote in her journal:

> *January 13–Friday the 13th*
> *I never have been superstitious but today was ridiculous! I ruin people's lives, including my own. I stayed at Wayne's till 1:30. Before that I got so many people upset with me. My Mom is so mad at me it is unbelievable. She cried a lot. She just can't believe I could be so horrible. I can't either. She cried "What good is life anyway? It's too hard, too hard." See, she'll probably have a nervous breakdown because of me. Why do I do this to her? It's not only her, it's my Dad too. They must wonder why I'm so bad. I guess they feel they made some error in my raising. I think it's just a flaw of character. Don't I love my parents enough to obey and respect them??? I need to change.*
> *And Wayne, he loves me I think. I don't ever want to hurt him. If I hurt one more person my mind will pop. I won't be able to live with myself. <u>I can't hurt Wayne!</u>*
> *I don't even know where all these words come from. I don't know if I believe them.*
> *I'm staying up all night or until I finish my college applications. It's 2:22 a.m. Actually, it's Saturday . . . I'm not going to bed . . .*

We treated Tracks like a hero, and rightly so. We'd snuck saucers of milk to her all week since her brave ride to town. Susan and I, acting in concert, would tiptoe into the kitchen and quietly fetch the saucer and the milk, working so quietly that even Tracks didn't wake up until we touched her. She liked to sleep in the far corner of the kitchen, at the base of the refrigerator where it exhaled warm air. We'd touch her, and she would snap out of sleep and look around for a second as if she didn't know where she was, then she'd see the milk and start to lap it. One time she didn't even stand up, just lay there drinking the milk that we had positioned in front of her.

I liked to think of her ride. What had she been doing on the roof of the car in the first place? Why hadn't Mom or Elizabeth noticed her there before they left for town? What mixture of joy and terror had been in her heart during the ride? And did she ever dream about it now? Did she remember it? Did she count it among her achievements? Because she should have.

Grandpa peered out the window, now that the light was rising, and tried to see if it was still misting or raining or sleeting—whatever it was that had made the gutters drip all night. He could see beads of water hanging from the clothesline.

A crow materialized out of the fog, winging fast across the yard, and faded away.

The back steps were just wet, not icy. He touched the grass with his toe—maybe a little icy. He noticed the Christmas tree still lying by the shed.

When he started the car, cold air surged from the vents. He turned off the fan. He had been going to Kansas City six days a week, so that by this point it felt normal. It was a commute.

The driveway seemed fine, and the gravel road was the same, so he was surprised when he approached the stop sign at the end of the road and his brakes locked up. He was sliding—ice, the road was coated with ice—and he wasn't going fast, but he wasn't slowing down, either, and he was about to slide right past the stop sign and across the blacktop.

A sick feeling of not having control.

Then, just as his car reached the blacktop, the tires regained their grip and stopped the car with its nose jutting into the road. The car was slightly askew—the tail had drifted out of line as it slid—and he pulled across the blacktop onto the continuation of the gravel road. He got out. He wanted to see. And he also wanted to breathe the air, and stand up. He felt addled, angry that he'd been careless, and glad no one had seen.

Indeed, the gravel was covered with ice. He walked to the blacktop. The blacktop had no ice. This happened. Sometimes the gravel roads were colder than the blacktops, or less frequently traveled, or not dusted with salt or sand, and they iced up more easily than the blacktops

The rest of the trip to Kansas City went fine. When he got there, Grandma was asleep. There was a stack of the day's new mail by her bed. Get-well cards. He began opening them, and as he did this she woke up.

She said, "I heard paper."

He kept a log of the visitors on the notepad at her bedside, as he did every day he was here. Clarice, who came after noon, also wrote in the log. There was a gift of four little round soaps that came with Clarice from Grandma's secret pal in the Extension Club. Clarice recorded this gift by drawing four circles. At the end of the day, this is what the notepad page looked like:

> Sat 21　　10 cards
> Belford　　gift - 0000 soap
> Clarice　　from Secret Pal, Valley Grove
> 13 letters from Ext. club
> Mary Helen　　Babe B.
> Clayton & Grace Kimmis
> Virginia Palmer
> Kent & L. called

That was her bedside notepad. In addition, Grandpa carried a pocket notebook with him. He had written his initials at the top: BGJ. On the back was a calendar for 1984 and 1985. Inside the notepad, the first page contained this, which he had written a couple of weeks ago:

> Tumor in neck
> Lymph nodes
> get some tissue
> Biggest danger could be paralyzed
> (operate 10 or a little later)

He also wrote many phone numbers in the booklet: Darrell, Darrell at work, Kent, Kent at work, Clarice, the church, the pastor, the bank, Emmett, Billie, and all the doctors, pages of them.

Then there was one page, written yesterday, that had just one word. It read: *pancreas.*

On Sunday, while Dad and Elizabeth were in Kansas City, Susan and Mom and I were spending the afternoon going about our own business. I was drawing at the kitchen table, creating what I was coming to consider a masterwork. I drew the desolate surface of a distant planet. I depicted the landing of a spaceship. The men from the ship walked to a door, the door led to a tunnel, the tunnel went down, and then the tunnel continued down onto another sheet of paper, and another, and another—the stairs, the ladders, the flat stretches, the elevators—until I had reached the point at which I ran out of room for all these connected sheets of paper on the table-top. I looked up, thinking of moving the entire thing to the floor, and I saw, out the kitchen window, the horses—shaggy and ruddy and really huge—grazing about twelve feet away.

"The horses are out!" I cried. The house gave nothing back. "The horses are out!" I said again. Then I heard footsteps upstairs and the sound of the desk chair rolling in the study.

"Where?" Susan asked from upstairs.

"Right by the kitchen," I said.

Mom came into the room. As soon as she saw the horses, she said, "Susan, put on your boots, quick."

Elizabeth was the best at handling the horses. Dad was second best. Susan and Mom were marginal. And without Elizabeth's guidance, I was basically incompetent on account of my fear of being kicked.

Still, at Mom's request, I put on my boots and went outside. The horses didn't even look up when we approached. They were enjoying the grass of the lawn.

"I'm not sure I know how to put this on," Susan said, untangling a halter.

We got the idea to lure them with oats. We filled two coffee cans halfway with oats and shook them and called the horses and the horses went for it. After all, it was winter, and though the grass in the yard was slightly green, oats were more appealing. We lured them back into their pasture.

How had the gate come unlatched? We didn't know.

Back inside, my cheeks still cold from the horse adventure, I saw my drawing on the kitchen table and I realized my enthusiasm for it had waned. I sat down. I would just go ahead and finish it. I drew a room at the bottom of the deepest tunnel, and when I was done with it I realized it was too small a room to warrant such a long passageway, but, well, maybe there was something about the room that made it more important than its size suggested. Something secret.

Pray

So Dad sat with her. He would drive up on Sundays, because that was the easiest day of the week for him to give to her, and because it was the day that Grandpa didn't come. (Church, home, church, home—such was Grandpa's Sunday.) Also, because of church, she got few visitors on Sundays, and therefore his company filled a void. Doctors were scarce, nurses were quiet, there were no tests, no consultations, nothing new. No mail, even. He would drive toward the city after breakfast, two hours through the countryside, then up the old Highway 50 into the gathering commotion of the city—the same way his family had always approached the city from Windsor—skirt the Country Club Plaza, head north a few blocks, and park in a hunkering garage. The coolness of that concrete structure. He'd step across the street. He'd ride the elevator, walk down her hallway. The babble of a television from another room. A nurse whose name he should remember.

He'd turn into her room. 1441. The winter sky seen through the window. Flower arrangements and fluorescent lights. A plastic pitcher of water.

So he sat with her. Five hours, six hours. Just the two of them. He hadn't spent this much time alone with her since ... since when? Had there even been such a time? When he was a baby, sure, and a toddler—though that didn't count, really. But he wondered how many times he'd talked to her as an adult for more than a few minutes without someone else intruding. The rare phone call when he happened to catch her alone; but even then Grandpa would pick up the other line as soon as he came in from doing the chores. During birthdays and Christmases she was entrenched in the kitchen, busy, aided by Mom and Lucretia, Billie and Clarice. And when her grandchildren were around, we were always the focus of her attention—rightly so. Perhaps if he caught her early—before we grandchildren were awake, while Grandpa was outside—and sat at the kitchen table with her, there would be a small space of time when it was just the two of them. It was brief, though, and at that point in the day she brimmed with plans and visions of how to organize the coming hours for her family, and therefore she was not inclined to relaxed conversations.

Not that she was in a state of mind for such interactions now. She was in pain. She was away from her land and house, away from the skies of home. But the two of them—mother, son—did have time, and so they talked. He asked her questions because he hoped it drew her away from the present. Distracted her. And he was curious, too, and concerned that anything left unsaid and unasked now might be lost. And his questions and her answers naturally and quickly retreated to places and times when she was young—before grandkids, before him, even before Grandpa—as if by inhabiting those times through speech and memory she was fleeing as far as she could from the dreadful present and yet remaining herself. Because she did remain herself, even in the face of what they hated to name aloud.

Most of what she said, he had never heard before.

When they still lived up north of Green Ridge in that little house, she just walked away one evening. She was four, and she just headed up the road. It was May. There was honeysuckle in the fencerow, and a big old bull cow was lying in the pasture looking as gentle as a rabbit.

Her mother saw her leaving and called up Aunt Lina and told her that a little girl was headed in her direction. Lina and Great-Grandma Calvert conferred, then Great-Grandma crept down to the road and hid back in the brush. She saw Mildred coming along. She wanted to be sure Mildred turned up their lane. Sure enough, she did.

Inside, Mildred played "Polly Wolly Doodle" on the piano, which was the only song she could play. She played it again. Then she asked for a treat. They gave her fresh bread with butter and sugar sprinkled on top. Then she said she felt like going home because she wondered if Baby Emmett maybe needed her, because probably he did.

At home, Mother gently asked her where she'd been. "Up the road," she said. "At first, I ran away. Then I was just visiting."

Later, fireflies came out. Emmett was asleep in his basket on the kitchen table. Mother washed Mildred's feet before bed.

Then afterward, at night—or sometimes at work the next day, during the waning minutes of his lunchtime—he would record what she had told him. Their Sunday talks. He would write down his memory of her memories, such as they were. He considered tape-recording their conversations and even brought a recorder to the hospital one day. But when he arrived, he realized the recorder's batteries were weak, and after a brief consideration of where he could buy batteries on a Sunday morning, he thought better of the whole endeavor. The machine in his hands belonged to the world of now and was too akin to the grim technology of the hospital. She'd never been comfortable with tape recorders, anyway. He left the recorder in the car.

His written notes of their talks, he knew, were imperfect representations of her words, which were imperfect representations of her memories, which were imperfect representations of events that had happened, things that had been said, and people she had known. Even so, he did what he could, listened to her words, and discovered that with some imagination, some intuition, and careful appreciation of the pauses within her telling, he could bridge the gaps—if momentarily—and glimpse the fullness and reality of the events being described. He could see her, young.

The hayloft window. At the farm at Bryson. It was just an opening in the side of the barn. She could dangle her legs over the edge, like sitting on the back of a buckboard wagon. Down below her, cows ambled in and out of the barn.

In the spring, this was the pasture where the calves were kept with their mothers. The sunlight would slant in the window. The dark calves would buck and bolt in the field. They would sniff the grass, not yet interested in eating it, but interested in being interested in it.

She also had a view of the apple orchard and peach orchard. Sometimes she saw Daddy walking across the pasture, or working the far field with the horses.

The hayloft window was a good place in the rain, too. She could watch the rain, but not get wet. Be warm in a pile of loose hay. The sound of the rain on the barn's tin roof. The smell of the enlivened earth.

So he sat with her, another evening, just hours after her second surgery, on a dark day which became a dark night. Grandpa and Kent had left half an hour ago, and since then she had seemed somewhat more comfortable, and also more quiet, probably because of the recent dose of painkiller, which was, he understood, a narcotic. He sat beside her. Her eyes had been closed for many minutes, and her breathing had slowed as if she was asleep. He held her hand. Watched the drip of the IV.

She was still wearing her neck cuff—a foam collar that immobilized her head—and it seemed unfair that she was still burdened with the paraphernalia of her first surgery now that she'd come out of her second surgery. Her hair hung loose and gray, no longer the carefully styled globe it had been for years. The hospital hadn't washed her hair once in thirty-eight days.

"Oh," Grandma said. She suddenly clenched his hand. Her face went rigid, eyes still shut. Her pain was coming back. She went silently through it, but gripped his hand persistently. After enough of this, he consulted with a nurse, who checked with the staff physician, who allowed Grandma's next dose to be moved up.

Dad noticed that a sweat had broken out on Grandma's forehead. He dabbed it with a moistened towel.

"Are you hot?" he asked.

"Feels good," she said.

When, at ten o'clock, he had to leave for the night, she had still not received her painkiller, nor her meperidine. He told her he was sure that when Daddy and Kent saw her in the morning, she would be feeling better. But he wasn't sure of that at all. What did he know? Then, after he kissed her goodnight, she looked up at him and said, "Pray for your poor mother."

He felt stunned as he walked away. His legs seemed hollow, and his eyes would not focus. As if this second surgery—the bad news it brought, the pain, the recovery to come—wasn't enough for her— for him, for everyone—now her parting words drew him along a new avenue of distress. He felt weak, walking through the nighttime hospital. He became lost, somehow ended up in the basement. Finally, he made it outside and walked toward the parking garage. The wind pushed against him from the north.

When Grandma had come out of surgery at noon, the surgeon reported that the disease had presented itself in an unexpected way: instead of being discrete and defined, it had infiltrated the wall of the stomach. This explained why radiology had failed to describe the problem there. The encased disease made the stomach rigid, unable to function, and made removal impossible. In the meantime, as they had discussed, a feeding tube had been inserted.

During all her weeks in the hospital, Grandma had rarely let her suffering be known to others. She kept it sequestered through force of will and personality and propriety. This was a way of protecting her family. For fifty years—her adulthood—she had been a wife, mother, grandmother, sister. A caregiver, comforter, protector. She had almost never, in all those years, let her own needs impose on anyone, but rather satisfied herself through the very act of tending to others. Whatever frictions were created by this way of living were addressed in ways that were not entirely known to Dad. Church, probably. Playing organ and piano, certainly. What else? The skies of the prairie? The companionship of her clubs and friends?

Tonight, though, he had seen the basic matter of her character break in the face of what she endured.

"Pray for your poor mother."

He drove on eastward into the night, toward home. The city

lights were removed to his rearview mirror, and then gone entirely. The road went from four lanes to two.

Once upon a time, he could have prayed for her. For most of his life, in fact, he'd been a Christian. He'd been so thoroughly Baptist that before entering the University of Missouri, he'd told a buddy that he sure hoped they didn't try to teach him all that evolution bunk. And he'd been offended when he visited a church affiliated with the American Baptist Convention—not his Southern Baptist Convention—and the preacher quoted Socrates.

As he drove, he remembered his cat named Puff.

When he was eleven, the farm's cat had disappeared. It was no great cause for alarm. She was a nameless mouse-catcher, shy tenant of the barn, patroller of the corn crib.

"Supposing a bear ate her?" Kent posed at the noon meal.

"Bears only live in the mountains," Darrell said.

Belford, spearing green beans with his fork, said, "Probably just coyotes."

"But I haven't heard coyotes in weeks," Darrell said.

Kent paused with his glass of milk held in both hands. "I remember when they came that one night when that calf was dead and they put up a whole mess of howling like you never did heared." He was breathless after this.

"Heard," Mildred corrected. Then she corrected herself. "Hear."

"Hmp," Belford said.

"Yeah," Darrell added, "a coyote can't do anything without yipping and howling and telling all of creation what he's up to." He didn't know this to be fact, but it sounded good enough to imply fact.

"They can eat a meal," Belford said, "without a peep. Unlike you two."

When lunch was over, Darrell took it upon himself to investigate the cat's disappearance. He found a good stout stick, walked down past the corn crib, stalked along the hedge, and crouched there, surveilling, thinking that the dastardly coyotes would surely show themselves. After several minutes passed with no hint of coyote, he reassessed his mission. He would seek the cat, not the coyotes.

Since the center of her territory was the barn, he went there and peeked into all manner of nook and crook—old milk cans, the collapsed feed trough, the cubbies where the ceiling joists rode over the beams. Upstairs in the hayloft, the sun chiseled through the cracks between the siding boards, and he heard a rustling in the hay. He found the cat tucked down in a cozy hay den, suckling five kittens.

Because his discovery of the kittens was part of their genesis, Darrell felt connected to them, and as the kittens grew, one became his favorite. He was a long-haired cat, white except for a red tail and a red spot on his crown—like a hat worn jauntily askew. He was a big tomcat with a broad nose and huge feet, but he was the sweetest, most affectionate cat you ever could meet. Darrell named him Puff, and he loved him. While the other cats—the whole skittish tribe of them—would scurry away if Darrell approached, Puff would walk directly toward him and speak what was clearly a greeting. He would flop down next to Darrell and purr the deep purrs of contentment, even before Darrell started petting him.

Then, when Puff was a year old, he got sick. He lay panting in the central walkway of the barn, near the door to the oat crib. Darrell would check on him several times a day, bring him water and food, sit with him. After a few days, Darrell started praying for Puff every time the clock in the front room chimed the hour or half hour. He felt that if he kept to this schedule, his prayers would accumulate. But eventually Puff stopped drinking water, his eyes moved sluggishly behind his half-closed inner eyelids, and he died.

Dad drove on homeward. Getting closer.

Now, Grandma knew that he didn't pray—that he wasn't a practicing Christian, much less a practicing Baptist. She knew that and was upset by it. His "heresy." And knowing his break with Christianity, her request that he pray for her was all the more painful.

When was the last time he'd prayed? After all, there had been a time when he'd been a professional prayer. At the start of his sopho-more year in college he'd felt called to the ministry, and while still in college he was ordained, and delivered two sermons a week at a little country church, even while he studied philosophy at school. His faith and philosophy informed each other, and he didn't think that rational arguments could affect his relationship with God. And maybe they didn't, but over time—in divinity school, graduate school, as a young professor—he found that he didn't believe in certain Christian principles anymore, such as life after death. These changes in him did not come about from active thought or consideration, but simply happened slowly on their own. And while leaving behind many of the central tenants of Christianity didn't bother him any more than leaving behind, say, a belief in the Easter Bunny, it became harder as his young family moved from town to town to find a church of like-minded people who were led by an intelligent minister—and how many small-town ministers, after all, were as intelligent as someone with three Yale graduate degrees?—and though for a long time he considered himself part Calvinist and part skeptic, there came a day, at Wooster College in Ohio—his fourth teaching job in six years—when a student conducting a survey of faculty members asked if he considered himself a Christian. He thought about it. He leaned back in his desk chair. Then, for the first time in his life, he said no, he was not a Christian.

That was ten years ago.

When he got home to our farm—after midnight—he pulled up behind the station wagon and turned off the engine. He thought to himself, Well, I prayed for Puff, didn't I? I prayed and prayed.

God, let Puff be well. God, let Puff live long. God, cure Puff. God, let Puff be happy again. God, protect Puff. God, preserve Puff. God, love Puff. God, bring Puff back to me. God, defend Puff from pain. God, help Puff be strong. God, don't take Puff from me.

Plans

After an energetic game of playground soccer on a generously warm early February Thursday, my classmates and I came back inside and mobbed the water fountain. It was just up the hallway from our classroom, and we were allowed to drink there without supervision before returning to the room. We were a thirsty lot. Toni was in front of me in line, and there was no one behind me. When Toni leaned over the spout, she held back her hair with one hand. Her face was gleaming from the exertion of the last half hour. She drank, and when she stood up, she looked at me—it was just the two of us—and said, "I hope your grandma gets better." Then she walked toward our classroom.

The truth of the matter was that I had broken up with Kathy Smith—not because of who she was, but because of who she wasn't. Kathy was a dynamic girl who had pulled me into her whirlwind. She had come out of nowhere, a new girl in a school where there were only a handful of new kids every year. She knew what was cool, looked somewhat like a dancer from a rock video, and was enthusiastic on the subject of me. She was so direct and vibrant that to say no to her required substantial effort. But there was no remedy for the fact that she was not Toni Renken.

Toni hadn't attended Russellville for kindergarten, and in first grade she was in the other class section, so I had no contact with her. In second grade, she was also in the other section, but we shared a recess period twice a week and at one point I noticed her running past me, on some urgent errand, and I registered her cuteness—and the fact that her brown pigtails were held by those little rubber-band ponytail holders that had two colored plastic marbles on them. These I considered extremely becoming. And Toni, I noted, was a good runner—and being a good runner was one of the yardsticks by which I measured people.

Third grade found Toni and me together, finally, in the same classroom. That was the year Craig Linhardt and I became interested in girls, before the other boys in our class. Yes, it was true that even with her doe eyes and warm spirit, Toni was our second choice. There was a girl named Michelle Marquis whom we adored foremost, and it seemed only natural that she and Toni were good friends, and that Craig and I were good friends, though it was never clear how the girls ranked us. The general understanding was that we all liked each other, though this was never actually said. We did choose to sit together when our teacher arranged us in four-desk clusters for a month. Also, there were some lively homemade Valentine cards passed between us that winter. This was what I wrote for Toni: *My nose may be runny, / I don't have much money, / but the world would be sunny, / if you'd be my honey.* I drew accompanying pictures of a runny nose, cash, the sun, and honey.

At the end of third grade, Michelle Marquis moved away. This was a maddening injustice and the cause of a few weeks of specific heartbreak and a summer of a more generalized sense of loss. I had dreams about riding the bus with her, laughing with her, then watching her step off the bus onto a dusty gravel road and knowing I wouldn't see her again. But as soon as school resumed—fourth grade, last year—the pain evaporated as it became apparent that Toni was more wonderful and radiant than ever, as if she were now Toni times two. For fourth grade, we ended up in the same class again, and that was the year we almost got married.

It was not my idea to get married. And it wasn't Toni's. What happened was that a couple of the girls in Toni's bevy of friends got the idea that a marriage at school would be an awfully fun thing to arrange and attend. They'd been watching soap operas over the summer.

I was for it. I mean, it would link me to Toni for the rest of my life. Perfect. Now, in discussing the wedding, I did not deal directly with Toni. I dealt usually with Jeena, one of Toni's friends. Jeena was smart and cordial, and we worked through the details of the wedding over the course of many recesses. Basically, it was her job to get me to agree to whatever the girls wanted, and I didn't mind doing so.

For example, she appeared on the sidelines of a recess kickball game one morning, and I excused myself and went over.

"We're trying to figure out where to hold the ceremony," she said.

I shrugged. "Shouldn't we have it here?" I said, meaning the playground/track area in general.

"Yeah, but where exactly?" she asked.

I looked around. "The middle of the field inside the track?"

She didn't acknowledge this suggestion. "There are three options," she said. "One: at the bottom of the big slide, and the guests could sit on the slope. Two: under the jungle gym because we could decorate the jungle gym. Or three: under the tree by the cafeteria."

"If we had it at the bottom of the slide, would Toni come down the slide?"

We laughed.

"Actually, the big tree by the cafeteria is what Toni wants," Jeena said.

"Okay," I said.

Eventually word came that it was time for me to propose, and that it would have to be done in person. This made me nervous. Here, the biggest moment of my life, and I actually had to ask her myself, and not via proxy, note, implication, or hand signal.

At the appointed time, I walked up to Toni, who was standing on the track with her hands clasped behind her back. We were within view of everyone. I stopped in front of her. She was looking down, scuffing the cinder track with her foot.

I said, "Toni, will you marry me?"

And she said, "I don't know. Let me go check." Then she walked up the slope to her cluster of girlfriends.

This was worrisome. Why had I been pushed to propose if the answer hadn't already been decided?

Toni came back a minute later. "My friends say that I should, so okay."

It was a sunny September day, and as I watched Toni walk back to her friends I knew that she didn't care a lick for this whole thing, and her indifference wicked the magic right out of it. Still, I was getting to marry her, wasn't I? I would take what I could get.

News spread. This kind of engagement was information that traveled fast. Susan found out. She told my parents and Elizabeth as we were all eating dinner one night. It was amusing to them, and my father asked a couple of questions about the legal nature of a playground marriage. I vigorously denied the engagement, which I realized was silly considering that I couldn't keep it secret once we were married. But out of context—away from school, away from the girls who bubbled with anticipation and importance and who were so pleased with my compliance—the whole thing felt silly, and made me feel exasperated and, considering Toni's coolness toward me, melancholy.

Still, there was a schedule to maintain. Oral invitations had been issued. We held a recess-time rehearsal under the elm tree. There was a nice, gentle slope there, and a good bit of shade. Jeena was Toni's stand-in for the rehearsal, and other girls filled various roles, such as bridesmaids, preacher, and flower girl. I didn't do much but stand wherever they told me to stand, and listen to them debate the finer points of what was involved in a wedding ceremony.

The final matter to discuss was the honeymoon. Toni's idea of a honeymoon was not to have one. But after some coaxing by her friends, and a bit of creative rephrasing, the deal we agreed on was this: Toni and I would walk one lap around the track, holding hands, and I would kiss her on the cheek at the end. Tasteful and romantic. So the last obstacle was cleared.

Always, Toni was easy to daydream about. It required no effort, and it felt natural. Toni did nothing in particular to encourage this, other than always seeming to hide part of herself from view of everyone. In other words, she had an inner life, and this was rare at our school, and bespoke intelligence. The other boys didn't understand this attribute, but I did.

Then, two days before the ceremony, I was on the swing set with a couple of younger kids when Jeena came over. I shooed the third graders away. Jeena sat on the swing next to mine.

"Toni called it off," she said.

"Why?" I asked. "I thought we agreed." Could she really cancel it at this late hour, after we'd done so much planning?

"We tried to change her mind," Jeena explained. "We really did, Jeremy. But she just doesn't want to do it."

Jeena stayed for another few minutes, trying to comfort me by being friendly. Then she went back to the girls, and I was there alone, and I did the only thing I could do at the moment, which was to swing as high as possible.

I shied away from Toni for the rest of fourth grade.

Being at the mall with Mom and Susan was always an exercise in frustration, and this night was no different. At the video game arcade, I had burned through my dollar's worth of tokens in about twenty minutes, even counting the time I spent trolling the rows of games, weighing my options. My game budget blown, I wandered back into the bright lights of the mall and went to the toy store, where Susan and Mom met me earlier than I had hoped and dragged me to the fabric store, where they took an incomprehensibly long time picking out fabric for a skirt. After that, we went to a clothing store that served teenage girls, and I stumbled around in a stupor—my legs feeling numb like they did whenever I went to museums—until, after trying on several things, Susan finally decided to buy a pair of socks, and then, standing at the checkout counter, I idly spun the little display of earrings and suddenly sort of woke up and looked at what was in front of me: a dainty pair of red enamel heart earrings on silver posts.

I could buy these for Toni.

Fifth grade was supposed to have been different. I had felt that

it would be different. I remembered the sense of potential at the beginning of the year. Mrs. Davis had filled us with exciting visions of
what wonderful things we would do. Above all, it was a new start
for Toni and me. Our class was so small that it felt more like a club
than a class. There was no way, in that tiny classroom, to get more
than about fifteen feet away from another person. And on that first
day of school, Toni had picked a locker just one away from mine. She
had done that.

I blamed myself for being sidetracked by Kathy Smith. I had
wasted months. But now it was Toni I thought about, and whom I
knew I would keep thinking about forever. Earlier today at the water
fountain, when she had wished my grandma well, I had been surprised by the gesture, the compassion of it, the suddenness. Usually,
with Toni and me, things went along without incident for weeks at
a time until some act of tenderness from her—a private smile, her
asking to be on the room decoration team with me, or her foot secretly resting beside mine under the art room table—would con-
firm, or at least not rule out, what I had been feeling between us. If
you connected the dots, you could begin to see the shape of Toni's
feelings for me. And now, staring at these earrings, I felt that if only
I made the right gesture, then things between us would head more
quickly than ever in the right direction. The earrings were so simple,
and the enamel was that piercing Valentine red that leaves no room
for ambiguity, and I knew that I had enough money in my pocket,
and though it was embarrassing to have to admit to Mom and Susan
what I was considering—whom I was thinking of buying these for—
and embarrassing to have to make the decision quickly, and in front
of an audience, and embarrassing to have to buy the earrings from
the saleslady who was older than Mom and who looked at my cash
suspiciously—it was the right thing to do, the right impulse, the right
time, and Valentine's Day was four days away. So, it was nervous-
making, but I did it, and it was done, and outside the mall, in the
parking lot, in the mild winter air, with my heart still beating high
within my throat, I stood by the back door of the station wagon with
my fingers on the handle, waiting for the door to be unlocked, and I

looked up at the splattering of stars visible through the light-murk of the city, and then, only then, did I allow myself, for the first time, to imagine Toni wearing them.

Susan was kind. That weekend, she helped me find a box. The earrings came mounted on a small plastic card about the size of a matchbook. I peeled off the price tag. The front of the plastic card was covered with gray fuzz. I ran my thumb over it several times. Susan found a box that a pair of her earrings had come in and said I could have it. It was the perfect size, with a soft bed of white batting inside for the earrings to rest on. Susan wrapped the box for me. Her wrapping skills surpassed mine by several degrees. We used simple red wrapping paper. I did not label the wrapped box. But inside I had put a tiny handmade card. It just said "from Jeremy."

I carried the box to school on Tuesday in the pocket of my jacket. I could hear the earrings faintly clicking against the lid of the box. I was also carrying my Valentine-card box and a thickish batch of Valentine cards for all of my classmates. It was customary to give a card to everyone in the class, and it was probably better that way—fewer hurt feelings and whatnot—but it did sort of undermine the whole fun of receiving a Valentine card. What did it mean, after all, that Jimmy Rademan gave me a card showing two cartoon bees in love and on the back had this printed: "Bee my Valentine?" It meant nothing, and that was the difficulty of the whole business of Valentine's Day: telling the difference between something and nothing.

In the early afternoon, as the hour approached when we were planning to do our card exchange, I decided that instead of handing the present to Toni, I would slip it into her Valentine box along with my card to her. That way, she would discover the earrings on her own. Everyone loves a surprise! Also, this was a good plan because it meant I wouldn't have to give the gift to her in person, which was just too much to ask—even in the name of love, even on the day of love—and thinking about it had given me a sour stomach, and made me uninterested in lunch.

My own Valentine box was fashioned to look like a computer. With Mom's help, I made a keyboard, CPU, and monitor, all fitted together into one unit. The keyboard had actual keys drawn on it, in the right places and everything, and the monitor displayed this program that I had written:

```
10 ROM ** THIS COMPUTER RUNS ON VALENTINES **
20 PRINT "ENTER VALENTINES ABOVE"
30 LET X = ♥
40 PRINT X                    ♥ ♥ ♥
50 GOTO 20                    ♥ ♥ ♥
60 END                         ♥ ♥
```

When the time came, I retrieved my batch of cards from under my desk. I also got the little gift and held it cupped in my hand, out of sight. We all got up and started milling around stuffing Valentine cards into each other's boxes. This was a traffic nightmare—fifteen of us heading in different directions, bumping into each other. There also wasn't much of an element of surprise to it all—you could see people putting cards into your box. You came face to face with Jennifer Meisel as you were trying to get to her box and you saw that in her hand she had your card and was headed for your box. That's the kind of scene it was. I tried to save Toni's card and gift for a good time—a time when she wasn't looking, when no one was looking— but I soon realized that was going to be impossible. In fact, by the time I actually delivered her card, Toni was sitting back down at her desk, and she watched me put the card into her box.

When the delivering was done, the boxes were opened, and the Valentines were unsealed and read. Mrs. Davis came around and gave each of us a cupcake. All the cards I got were store-bought. The ones from the boys were usually signed with just the boy's name. The one from Mitchell was signed "your friend Mitchell." I appreciated that. The inscriptions on the cards from girls sometimes evoked the word "friend," but also words and phrases like "special" and "fun guy." The one from Toni was a generic-looking card with hearts on

the front, and on the back there were no preprinted words. Toni
had written her name and drawn a heart. That was it. At first, it was
sort of a letdown, but then I decided that it was actually, possibly,
a straightforward declaration of love. Nicely understated. No need
to fuss with words when a simple heart would do. Then I noticed
Mitchell's card from Toni. He sat right next to me, and I could see
that Toni's card to him had the exact same thing as mine.

I took the little red gift home with me that afternoon.

Deep: Part Two

Mildred woke up to find the window glowing like the minute before sunrise. She blinked at it, then realized there was movement in the house. She heard the back door close downstairs. She sat up and just then the door of her bedroom opened and she saw Mother and Mother said, "I see we woke you." Mother explained that there was a grass fire on the other side of Bryson and that Daddy and Uncle Garland had gone to help. Emmett was still asleep. It was the middle of the night, and Mildred and Mother went into the backyard and looked at the orange sky to the west. Curiously, they didn't smell smoke. Mildred looked at the end of the porch in the strange, false dawn light and saw that the place where Trixie slept was empty.

Later, after sunup, she and Mother took biscuits, apples, and water over to Bryson. The smoke was mostly gone, and when they got closer and saw the blackened fields, they also saw the men clustered around something and then they realized what the men were looking at: the remains of the schoolhouse. Mildred fought to keep from crying; she thought she would never get to go to school again.

They found Daddy up the road where he had helped keep the fire from reaching a barn. Trixie was with him. He said she'd followed him everywhere while he was beating at the grass fire. He said she'd barked at the fire because she knew it was bad. The crown of Daddy's straw hat was ringed with sweat and his eyes were bloodshot.

In the span of twelve days, they rebuilt the school. The new school was a lot like the old one, but with more windows and a flagpole. The school's lawn remained black through the autumn and was covered with *white in the winter, but when spring came it showed itself as a green thing again.*

It had started snowing around noon, but lightly, and off and on—as the forecast had suggested it might—and Mom wasn't concerned about it. She had brought Susan to Kansas City because she could see that Susan had been worrying about Grandma's illness—fretting over it, holding her fears too tightly—and she figured it would help Susan to see Grandma in person, to see for herself what was going on. The cruel imps of reality were rarely as fearsome as the hobgoblins the imagination could concoct. Susan needed this. Besides, Elizabeth had visited Grandma last month, and it had been good for both of them—grandmother and granddaughter.

For a time, after Mom and Susan returned from lunch, Grandma insisted that she must be getting a new roommate because she saw clothes hanging behind the door. It was just shadows, though, combined with the confusion of a pharmaceutically addled mind. She also talked about hearing strange noises in the heating system, as if the heating system had moods. But despite these blips, her lucidity and personality were intact—Grandma was still Grandma—and she admitted that she was feeling better than she had since before the second surgery, and she listened to Susan relate the tale of the day that Mom drove Elizabeth to school one morning not long ago, and how Elizabeth got out of the station wagon in front of the school, only to find Tracks scrunched up on the luggage rack, having made a six-mile trip from home. Grandma smiled at the right places. Susan drew a picture of Tracks on Grandma's bedside notepad. As she did this, Grandma began to worry out loud about the snow—that it was really coming down now, and that they should get started home. It was as if all the constellations were still in place: here was Grandma worrying about their safety. For Susan's benefit, and to take Grandma's mind off the present, Mom prompted Grandma to recall snowstorms from her childhood, but Grandma shook her head, and said, "Oh, I don't know. I don't remember anything specific."

"There must have been some fierce winds out there in the winter," Mom said.

"I do remember the wind," Grandma said.

In the late morning, Grandma had told them of the time the Bryson schoolhouse burned down. But that story, Mom recalled, arose from Grandma naturally, and she couldn't force her to produce another tale. Grandma was wearing out, and the snow wasn't letting up. They said goodbye earlier than planned.

After they'd gone, the hospital seemed quieter than it ever had. There was something about the snow that just hushed everything. Plus, it was a Sunday, so there were few visitors and few doctors. Mom and Susan had been her only company of the day. She'd had the room to herself since her last roommate checked out five days ago. She looked at the picture Susan had drawn for her: the black cat sitting on a pole-top bird feeder, looking at a bird on a branch nearby. Susan had written "Keep humming!" at the top.

The nurse brought her some raspberry Jell-O at four o'clock, and it was a flavor she hadn't had in a long time. She savored it, and listened to the buzz of the fluorescent lights and looked out the window at the snow.

The heating system started clicking. It was familiar. Then began small puffing noises that sounded like venting steam. These were intermixed with the clickings, and the two seemed to be coordinated, and after a while the puffs began to sound almost like words. "I knoooow *(click click)* this much *(click)* I knoooow *(click click)* this much *(click)*." Then came a pause before the pattern repeated.

Darkness came. The window went black. She asked a nurse if it was still snowing. The nurse didn't know, but several minutes later she returned and set a paper cup at Grandma's bedside. The cup was full of snow.

None of this was forecast, Mom kept thinking as she and Susan drove eastward through the steadily falling snow, and at first this thought was comforting—reassured her that the squall would blow

over—but soon she recognized that this was a storm, and whether it
was a minor storm or a major storm it would likely be with them for
the rest of the drive. They got out of the city all right. The roads were
just wet. The ground wasn't frozen and the snow melted upon landing. But east of Raytown they started plowing through slush, then
more slush—she felt like she was piloting a boat—and the darkness of night came early. At least they were in the little car—with
its front-wheel drive, its stick shift, its sure-footed demeanor—and
it soldiered on, trouper that it was, slush or no slush, darkness or
no darkness, come what may, come what might, but nothing about
the trip was easy—the endless slush, the spray from passing trucks,
headlights in the mirrors, her palms sweaty on the steering wheel—
and after they gassed up in Sedalia, the snow began coming down
more heavily, and it was accumulating, too, and that's when Mom
started calculating the remaining miles, and how long it would take
them to get home at forty-five miles an hour, then—just a few miles
later—redoing the calculations for forty miles an hour. Finally she
was forced into third gear and stopped trying to do math. Gone was
the slush; now it was snow they were driving through. They joined
a long line of traffic, creeping along—semis, pickups, cars—and
found some comfort in numbers, and a feeling of solidarity. Even in
this caravan, as it were, it was hard to tell sometimes exactly where
the road was. It was just a packed ribbon of snow. Were they driving on the shoulder or was this the road? The long hills were the
worst. The big semis crept up them, slowing everyone down, and
she waited all the while for the moment the little car would lose its
traction. It didn't, though. The air streaming from the car's defroster
vents carried the scent of diesel exhaust, but when they closed the
vent, the cabin of the car fogged up, so they went back to the diesel
fumes. At such slow speeds, snow settled on the hatchback window
and the rear defroster couldn't melt it quickly enough and therefore
soon there was no visibility out the rear window. Her side mirrors
were clotted with snow, and she rolled down her window to wipe
the left mirror clean. Overall, it felt like the world was closing in on
them: the darkness, the way the headlights couldn't penetrate the

falling snow, the covered hatchback, the diesel stink in their nostrils, and the sense—no, the reality—that the closer they got to home, the slower they went.

Her junior year of high school in Windsor, she roomed with Dorothy Botts. One noontime, they went home for lunch—they cooked it themselves— and that's when the snow started. They sat eating toast and fried eggs at their little table by the window and they could feel the temperature in the room dropping. The room was unheated, and they were glad that it was Friday, and therefore wouldn't be spending the night here. By the time they walked back to school, the sidewalks were so slippery, they held on to each other to stay upright.

Uncle Garland showed up at the door of Mildred's classroom half an hour before dismissal. He was anxious to catch the earlier train to Bryson. Mildred said goodbye to Dorothy and left with her uncle, dis- appointed because she and Dorothy had planned to buy cinnamon rolls at the bakery—a treat they allowed themselves only once a week—before parting after school.

At the depot, they were told that the line to Bryson had been blocked by a locomotive with a broken wrist pen, and that it would be late evening before it could be cleared. So they walked. The most direct route was the railroad, so that's what they took. Soon they were out in the countryside, though by then the snow was falling so thickly they couldn't see more than several paces in any direction. Mildred's feet grew cold, and little balls of ice clung to the hem of her long coat. The raised bed of the rail- road, combined with the fact that they couldn't see the fields on either side of them, made it seem as if they were crossing a long bridge. The going was slow, and the journey began to feel treacherous. It would be dark before long, and they had no light.

Finally, they were getting close to home territory, approaching the small towns that Russellville competed against in sports. There was solace in this—they knew these names, these schools, their gym- nasiums and tracks—but the relief of familiarity was offset by the fact that the roads were getting still worse, that Mom was down into second gear now and had no sense of the road beneath her. She knew that more and more it was not a matter of skill and patience that was bringing them through, but luck, just luck. The traffic had thinned. Nearly disappeared, in fact. People were pulling off. People were giving up. Cars were sliding into the ditches.

East of the little burg of Syracuse, the road was like a canyon: there was a high wall of plowed snow on each side. That's where the car started to move in a way that was not consistent with conventional forward movement. Nothing provoked the tail of the car to rotate in the opposite direction of the nose—no jerked steering wheel, no spinning drive-wheels, no bump or obstacle or patch of slushy hydroplaning. It just happened because it was bound to, and it started slowly, announcing its intentions, giving them time to picture the coming ballet, and then it was upon them, and the world was turning smoothly and somewhat majestically outside their windows, the headlights were shining against a wall of snow—blindingly—and Mom took her hands off the steering wheel and said calmly to Susan, "There's nothing I can do," and Susan was dumbstruck, imprisoned in the moment, astounded, but the words that were in her mind, but trapped, were "Well, you could *try!*"

The spinning and sliding ended. The car stopped. They were turned around in the road, facing the way they'd come. The whole maneuver had been rather neatly accomplished. It hadn't been jarring, or happened too quickly. There'd been no oncoming traffic, and no one behind them. The car's engine was still purring. Mom put the car into gear, drove back into Syracuse, tooled around a block in order to turn around, and headed toward home again.

Ten minutes later, they considered stopping at the Twin Pines Motel in Tipton, but their mishap had somehow hardened them, and they could visualize their destination so clearly now that to stop would be to endure an acute form of denial. So they continued.

It was difficult to measure their progress. With snow so thick around them and the murk of the coming darkness growing steadily, Mildred realized it was possible they might wander right through the little town of Bryson without even realizing it—not being able to see the buildings from the track.

Suddenly, out of the whiteout loomed the black iron of the disabled locomotive, sitting quiet and cold. They walked alongside. Garland called, but no one answered. There were no visible footprints in the snow. Behind the engine were two empty cattle cars. That was all. They kept walking, and Mildred looked back after a few seconds, and the train was already hidden in the storm.

If Highway 50 had been bad, Route U was horrible—completely unplowed, covered with seven or eight inches of snow and a few unhelpful and meandering wheel tracks. Somehow, though, they made it up the big hill by the Strobels' house, and somehow they made it through the sharp turn above the river without sliding down the embankment. They were so close now. The final hill on Mount Hope Road—that sharp little hill on the curve—was the worst yet, and the car spun all the way up it, and there was a moment then when it seemed as if they had stopped traveling forward and were in fact sliding backward. But it was an illusion caused by the direction the snow was falling, and they made it up the hill, and then reached the end of the driveway. They got out, locked the car, and headed over the hill on foot.

It was almost completely dark when they reached a crossing. Tracks in the snow showed that a wagon pulled by two horses had passed over the railroad tracks not long ago. Without the disturbed snow, they never would have realized it was a crossing.

Garland wasn't sure where they were. He looked one way, then the other. There was nothing to be seen. "This may be the lane down by the Perry place," he said. If that was the case, they were still a good way from home.

There wasn't a single tree or signpost or other distinguishing mark. Mildred pictured the crossing they wanted—southwest of the farm—and pictured the Perry crossing, trying to remember any difference between the two.

"Let me look," she said. She trudged away from the tracks. Soon she was standing alongside the remnants of last summer's vegetation, bent low by the snow. She reached to lift one of these forms. A thorn pricked her finger.

She returned to Uncle Garland. "This is our crossing," she said. "Those are the blackberry canes we pick in July. There aren't blackberries by the Perry place."

Over the hill, that last little journey. Snow in their shoes. Susan followed Mom, stepping carefully into her footprints. They couldn't see beyond their own feet, but they could feel the slope of the land. They crested the hill, went along a ways, then they were headed down, and then they hit the driveway, and followed it, then cut through the front yard, saw the lights of the house—finally—and looked in the kitchen window to see Elizabeth, Dad, and me all in there, just about to sit down to supper.

In the darkness, they followed the fenceline, then turned north. Uncle Garland started wondering aloud what kind of supper they'd be enjoying soon, naming every kind of food and drink he knew: cobbler, stew, roast beef, sausage, biscuits, beans, canned peaches, cornbread, preserves, milk, fried chicken, pie, coffee, dumplings, cookies, mashed potatoes, bacon, soup, cake. . . . He went on and on, while Mildred followed every word he said, picturing a tremendous feast, and in this way the last half mile of their trek went quickly, and they were suddenly standing on the back porch, stomping their feet.

After dinner, we sat around the wood stove. Just yesterday, Mom reminded us, she had been in the garden planting seeds. She'd put in rows of beets, kale, collard greens, spinach, radishes, and lettuce. It had been a warm day, at the end of a warm month—more like April than February—and the soil had been dry enough to work. She'd even uncovered earthworms.

As I lay in bed, I thought about those little seeds lined up under half an inch of dirt and ten inches of snow, and also the way the snow was still coming down. I pictured the car at the end of the driveway, covered with snow. I pictured the cows in the barn, huddled. I pictured Teddy asleep in his doghouse.

In four days, I would be eleven. In four months, it would be summer.

It snowed through the night and on into Monday. School was canceled. Dad stayed home, too. Then, in the late afternoon, just as the snow ended the wind kicked up, blew through the night—from the east instead of the west—and we woke on Tuesday to find two- and three-foot drifts blocking the driveway. A morning expedition comprising Dad, Susan, and me trekked through the woods, sheltered from the wind, to the end of the driveway, where we discovered that no mail had come Monday or Tuesday. Mount Hope Road was unplowed, but around noon we received a call from some neighbors telling us that two road graders had finally broken through the drifts at the top of Buhr's hill. The road was open. Just after getting that news, our lights blinked out, and we sat there waiting for them to blink back on, but they didn't, and Mom went to the sink and began drawing water. Without electricity, our well pump wouldn't work, and therefore we had to use whatever pressure remained in the holding tank to stockpile drinking water. We filled two pitchers, a one-gallon jar, a mixing bowl, and a bucket. We started feeling thirsty.

We all slept in the study that night. We arranged couch cushions and sleeping bags on the floor, and camped out near the wood stove—the house's only source of warmth. I woke up at one point and saw Dad putting more wood into the stove. His face was lit by the red glow of the embers, and then he closed the stove's door, and his face disappeared, and the room was dark again, and I heard him climb back into bed.

Winter pulls you backward, Dad thought. He lay next to the windows. The cold was creeping in, and the wood stove was struggling to keep the study warm. He hoped the big gnarled piece of oak he'd just added to the fire would improve things.

Winter pulls you backward, he thought again, but he didn't know where this idea came from or what it meant. He couldn't think clearly about it. He sensed a meaning in the words, but not one he could articulate.

He lay there in the stillness. He remembered that when he was a boy he could not go to sleep until every light in the house was turned off. He would lie in the bedroom waiting, listening to his parents moving about the house, the murmur of their voices, the click of the radio being turned off, the sound of water as his mother washed her face, the door of the icebox closing, his father's cough. The lights in the kitchen went out first, then in the living room. Finally, he waited for the last light, in the front bedroom, to go out. Then, only then, could he close his eyes and relax.

This night, this storm, this coldness. It didn't seem as if the drifts would melt for at least a week. They'd be snowed in for a while. That, and the electricity being out. The cattle and horses would be getting low on water soon.

Letting go is not instantaneous, he reflected. It is a process that has many compartments, none of which suggest what is coming next, none of which point you in any direction. This uncertainty made the journey more horrible than it already was. He was thinking of this not in the sense of letting go of her, of Grandma—that was a point he had not reached yet—but of letting go of hope. Hope that she would ever be well again, that she would ever be unburdened in this world. He was letting go of hope.

There was no one to tell him, *Now do this, now do that, now rest, now begin again.* No one to say, *Now you are done, you have done it well, you have done it correctly, now be peaceful.*

Go Back Tomorrow

The summer after her only full year of college, Mildred played piano for the movies in Green Ridge, a few miles from her parents' home. The movies were on Saturday nights. Mr. Hartley and a boy would set up the screen, projector, and chairs in the park by the railroad. The last thing they did was roll the piano across the street and onto the lawn. If the ground was soft from rain, they would lay down planks for the piano to roll on.

The people would come, paying ten cents apiece, and when the sky was dark enough, Mr. Hartley would start the projector, and Mildred would play. During the first minutes of playing, she would feel awkward, like she was part of a machine that wasn't properly synchronized, but soon she would find a natural rhythm in the music and in herself. There was a way that the music flowed out of her, easily, without having been generated by thought or toil, and in this there was satisfaction. The last scraps of sunset in the west would seep away, the moon would shine, clouds would roll along, and moths would hurl themselves at the bright eye of the projector and cast fluttering shadows onto the screen. After the movies were done, Mr. Hartley would drive her home in his Model T, always stopping to tell Mother and Daddy how she'd played with admirable energy and to standards that would satisfy the Maker.

Near the middle of the summer, though, she was stepping out of Sunday morning church service when she saw Bernice Wells, her former piano teacher, walking purposefully toward her in the foyer.

Bernice said, "Mildred," and latched onto Mildred's elbow with one hand. With her other hand she pointed at Mildred.

"I hear now that you're playing for the picture shows," she said. Mildred opened her mouth to respond, but Bernice went on: "and I don't esteem such music as exclaiming the glory of our Lord. Just consider those rag-a-tag notes echoing all the way up to heaven and tell me that it's something a young lady should be playing, much less playing for wages. I always warned you that you play too much like Hi Ki Griefe with all his floundering around, playing by ear, playing without calm intent or dignity, but in service of himself and profit. I hope you reconsider how you use the talent our Maker granted you. And tell your grandmother I send my regards."

She did play for the movies the rest of that summer, but that was the end of it. Yes, when she was back in Warrensburg at college she would play for breakfast at the hotel, and also the city paid her to play the piano on Saturday nights, music that was broadcast over speakers throughout downtown. But she considered these to be respectable engagements. Not that she had taken Bernice's reprimand too seriously—Bernice Wells had always been like the hen who complains loudly about the sudden and mysterious appearance of her own eggs—but it did make her think. And she did begin to realize that her abilities at the piano were a gift.

So there was music, always, and the high, crowning sky, and a sense of God's providence, and the old rose bush rambling and blooming throughout the whole summer. Yes, she did know who Belford Jackson was. His family attended the First Baptist Church, like hers, and though she didn't know him well she had always noticed, with satisfaction, the way he wore his Sunday suit—without looking hot or uncomfortable like most young men. He was taller than most, and she remembered seeing him play on the basketball team a few years ago, outjumping every opponent with ease. Yes, she would accompany him to the show in Sedalia that weekend. He picked her up in a 1933 Chevrolet he'd just bought, and outside the theater in Sedalia he lit a cigarette and she told him that she thought smoking was a terrible habit and that she wouldn't abide it. He snuffed the cigarette out and threw his remaining cigarettes into the bin.

This was just before Christmas, 1934—her third year of teaching at Bryson—and she found herself thinking of Belford during lessons, and while cooking, and almost any other part of the day during which she was supposed to be focusing on other tasks. He gave her a watch for Christmas and a funny card on which he had tallied the number of hours since they had started dating (455), and she checked his math and found it to be correct, and later she asked him why he had asked her out. He didn't want to answer at first, but she pressed him, and he said that he'd grown tired of dating unimpressive girls and decided to ask out the nicest girl around— that was her.

That winter, after returning from a Saturday show at the Tower Theater in Kansas City, she said goodnight and went inside, but after only minutes there was a knock on the back door, and it was Belford, who said his car wouldn't start. Belford, Emmett, and Uncle Garland went outside to look at the car, but they soon returned. It was decided that Belford would sleep in Emmett's room.

She lay awake that night, realizing that this was the first time she and Belford had slept under the same roof, and she wondered, dizzyingly, how many more such nights the future held.

On a late March afternoon, Grandpa drove Grandma into Sedalia to the hospital, where she was to start another round of chemotherapy. It was a cool day, but the sun was shining—it was the spring equinox, after all—and the sunlight had a promising warmth. It was the time of year in Missouri when you could begin to sense the approach of summer, and when the scent of the enlivened earth could be inhaled all the way to your core, where it fixed a certain stillness into your being. The sunlight felt good on Grandma's skin, and the warmth of Grandpa's new car, which had been parked in the sun, was like the enfolding heat of an incubator.

They drove north past the bare fields, crossed the railroad tracks, turned west on Highway 50, and headed into Sedalia. She felt the

freedom of it. She felt it fully, distinctly. Here she was, with her husband, outside, moving through the landscape, driving in his car for
the first time in nearly three months, and she enjoyed it, soaked it in
just like she was soaking in the sunlight. It was not difficult for her to
forget, momentarily, the state of her health, her lack of hair, the medical bills, the pain, the strange rooms she had spent so many weeks in,
the fuzzy, low-hanging cloud of Demerol, the strange meals, the bad
air, the nurses who were familiar with her private functions, the pills
and machines and schedules that bracketed her. In other words, the
whole of what she did was forget. That was what made the drive good.
She rode in the car. She rode with her husband on the first day of
spring. This sun, this moment, this man, these passing scenes were all
she let occupy her mind. The car rode gracefully, Grandpa drove well,
they talked of spring, of the grand old houses along East Broadway,
how she had always liked this wide street, those long porches.

This town where they had come on their first date.

It was a short ride. In the coming days, there would be more rides
like it, though not as refreshing as the first one. They repeated the
route on the 22nd, then again on the 29th.

On her bedside notepad on the day of the first ride, Grandpa
wrote that she received 12 cards that day—for a running total of
690—and that he'd been her only visitor of the day—which was un-
usual in Sedalia, where she often had a dozen visitors a day—and
then he added this at the bottom:

Mildred sure enjoyed car ride
said this car sure rides nice.

Early in April, Mom had been in the room alone with Grandma and
Grandma said, "I love you." Mom said, "I love you, too, Mildred. We
all love you." Declarations of love were extremely rare in our family,
and Mom could see that for Grandma to say it indicated a recogni-
tion of the reality of her situation. Then Grandma said, in a different
voice, the voice of someone lost in a dark wood: "What am I going
to do about my house?"

It was an appeal from one woman to another. Grandma knew that she would never return to her house, or if she did, however briefly, she wouldn't be able to maintain it with anything close to the vigor and thoroughness that had made it a happy and complete home for decades. She was worrying about her livelihood, her life, her husband, her body—all of these things at once—and this was the way she said it: "What am I going to do about my house?"

Backward

My dreams that spring, my little fantasies, all dissolved into vapor when confronted with the facts and limits of reality.

My Pinewood Derby car was born from an aspiration to build the sleekest, thinnest wedge of a car possible. I drew up some plans using a drafting board that Grandma and Grandpa had given me for Christmas. I drew the plans to scale, and they were beautiful. Dad and I transferred my design onto the wood, then cut the block carefully, then sanded the remaining sliver smooth. It was coming alive! It would clearly slip through the air much more quickly than last year's car, which, to be honest, had been designed with no aerodynamic principles in mind, but simply to resemble the spaceship in the video game *Defender*.

I picked out the glossiest neon-orange spray paint available, and the paint made the car. The paint glimmered and suggested speed. This parcel of plasma! This spark of tomorrow!

If there was one night of the year that all Cub Scouts looked forward to more than any other, Pinewood Derby night was it. It made up for a year's worth of the low points of being a Scout, be they boring (lectures on citizenship), frustrating (tales about some Scouts in another state who made five thousand dollars collecting aluminum scrap), harrowing (any talent showcase), insulting (flag-folding ceremonies botched by the youngest Scouts), or embarrassing (flag-folding ceremonies botched by my own den).

When you entered the school cafeteria, just seeing the wooden racetrack for the first time in a year had a way of stealing your breath away. The track was a long blond lick of plywood with two raised rails for lanes. The cars straddled those rails. The starting gates were about five feet off the ground and from there the track sloped down to a long flat stretch.

I had one of the best-looking cars, clearly, so it was just a matter of letting the car do its thing. My first match was against my pal Brad, and his car looked pretty goofy and chunky and had a sticker of the Dixie flag. I had total confidence in my car's ability to trounce such a jalopy.

My car lost three out of three races against him.

I lost my consolation match, too, proving that my car was going nowhere fast. What had gone wrong? I'd used a *drafting board* to design this car! I'd made the car so thin and aerodynamic that if I'd removed much more wood it would simply have been a graham cracker on wheels.

It was just before my car's last race of the night that I noticed something was awry. With the cars side by side at the starting line, I could see that the wheels on my car were set farther back than the wheels on my opponent's car. After the race, I started comparing, silently, the position of my wheels to those on other cars, and my suspicion was confirmed.

I had built my car backward.

Although the extent of my knowledge of engineering and physics made it difficult for me to judge exactly what performance issues a backwardly built car would endure, I did know enough to reach the conclusion that probably the car would have been better off built the normal way.

Last year, my spaceship car had done so well I had advanced to the races in Jeff City. This year, I ended near the bottom of the Russellville tournament, and though I got a blue ribbon, it was simply a ribbon for participation.

Then, a couple of weeks later, as if to prepare us for the huge step sideways that would be the move from Cub Scouts to Boy Scouts, our pack's Boy Scouts extended to us a warm invitation to join them for a campout. This was the kind of stuff we had been looking forward to for a long time. I, for one, already had a copy of *The Official Boy Scout Handbook,* and it contained a great deal more interesting things than our Cub Scout handbook did. For example, it explained how to build fires, make rope bridges, tell the difference between red-fox poop and gray-fox poop, improvise a tourniquet, navigate by the stars, and treat chemical burns. Whereas we Cub Scouts spent most of our meetings in the school cafeteria eating Fudge Stripes cookies, the Boy Scouts, I knew, spent their time adventuring and saving lives.

But, but, but. It turned out the campsite was in a field by a gravel road. It was somebody's pasture, with old cow pies to prove it. And the camping equipment was a bunch of old National Guard surplus—huge canvas tents, a double-burner propane stove, and a kitchen sink setup with gas burners to heat water for washing dishes.

We helped set up the bivouac. We hoisted our tent. We dug a little trench around the tent to collect water if it rained. We waited for the fun to begin, but it kept being delayed. A few of the best Scouts weren't on this particular campout, but Lyndell Whittle was there, and we stuck close to him until he headed out into the woods and explained to us that he needed to be alone on his mission. It made sense—he didn't want a pack of ignorant boys crashing through the woods while he was hunting or tracking or scouting or whatever it was he was doing. Later, we followed another Boy Scout into the woods, only to learn he was looking for dead grapevines because, he said, you could smoke dead grapevine just like a cigarette.

Back at camp, for dinner, most of the Boy Scouts had brought bologna sandwiches and bags of chips and sodas.

Then we were put on dishwashing duty.

In the tent, the night went from cool to cold, and the inadequate insulating properties of my sleeping bag soon became evident. I lay shivering, awake, late into the night, listening to the dull silence around me and the occasional pickup passing on the gravel road, and

I checked my watch and it was just after midnight—which meant it was no longer March, but April.

The next weekend, the seeds Mom had planted in February started to come up. I saw them first—little nubs of green—and went and got Mom and she came outside and was so happy to see these seeds coming up and I asked her to remind me what exactly these seeds were and she said beets, radishes, spinach, buttercrunch lettuce, kale, and collards, and I realized, oh great, not a single thing to eat.

I still had the little red heart earrings, the ones I had failed to deliver to Toni on Valentine's Day. With the spirit of springtime stirring within me, I got the notion to give them to her on her birthday, in the middle of April. This time, I felt, I would be able to go through with it. Valentine's Day was too loaded. Giving her a gift on her birthday would be easier, yet would deliver the same message.

I unwrapped the earrings. The bright-red wrapping paper wouldn't do. I opened the box and looked at the earrings for the first time in two months. They were as pretty as before. I read the tiny note that was in the box. It just said "from Jeremy," so I left it in there. I rewrapped the box in some blue paper with tiny yellow dots.

It was my burden, that little box, and also my hope. It was a seed of sorts—a small thing that contained the potential to create something new. Again I carried the box to school, but upon entering the classroom and seeing Toni there taking off her jacket, I knew that again my task was impossible, and I carried the earrings home at the end of the day.

Why did something so simple prove so difficult? I recognized that there was a bundle of emotion and thought and creativity in my mind—a sense of potential that was mine and mine alone—and that it was this package—this bit of me—that I really wished I could give to Toni. If I could show it to her, share it with her, she'd understand how I felt about her, and why I felt that way about her, and why it was the right thing for her to feel the same way about me, and then everything would be neatly tied up. Everything would be understood. The earrings were just things, but they were trying to express all this stuff, and if I was so weak that I couldn't even give the earrings to her, then how would there ever be any way I could get her to understand the rest? And what was in her mind? And what if she felt the same way that I did, or at least a similar way, but she was also stopped cold by the inability to share it with me. How would we ever know how the other person felt?

It was frustrating. It was self-complicating.

Sometimes, too, you got what you wanted and then it turned out not to be what you wanted in the first place. So there was that to think about, too. How much of what I thought I wanted was not what I wanted at all? It sapped my core to try to think about that. I mean, I knew I wanted to be with Toni, that was not in question. But what would that actually be like? Similar precedents were not promising. Like Boy Scouts, which had proved to be infected with the same pettiness and total lack of imagination that Cub Scouts carried. Or guitar lessons. I'd been playing guitar for over a year, but I was no nearer to becoming a rock star than before I started. True, I knew twelve chords. And "Ring of Fire" was an excellent song, and so was "Ghost Riders in the Sky." But one time when I was at Brad's house his cousin had left an electric guitar there and I had picked it up and realized I didn't even know how to turn it on. So, what the heck, you know? Where was I headed with my guitar teacher, Darlene, and her honky-tonk songs? That's the kind of thing that was maddening. I had wanted to learn guitar. Okay, fine. I learned guitar, but then it turned out not to be the thing I'd pictured. If things never turned out how I pictured them, then what was the point of picturing them in the first place? But without picturing things, how was I supposed to even have a life? I spent a lot of my time picturing things, but what did it gain me? If picturing things was more rewarding than actually attaining them, then why even try to pursue your dreams?

After Christmas, I saw Grandma one time. It was in the middle of March, and she had been moved from Kansas City to a nursing home in Sedalia. My family, all five of us, drove to Sedalia after school on

a Wednesday and went to the nursing home. The place was about
half a mile off the highway, a bit east of town, surrounded by stubbly
cornfields. I had been told in plain terms that her move to the nursing home was not a sign that she was getting better, and I had also
been warned that she would be wearing a wig because the treatments
had left her bald. We all gathered in her room—Grandpa was already
there—and said hello, and one by one we stood beside her bed and
talked. I was the last to go, and I could tell that she was different, that
her face was more narrow, and that she had no makeup on and there
was a flatness in her eyes. I went to her bedside and took her hand
and said hello and she said she was happy to see me and I said that I
was happy to be there, and Grandpa huffed and said, "Don't just hold
her hand! She's your grandmother!" and so I leaned in to hug her,
which was difficult because she couldn't raise herself from the bed. I
worried that somehow I would hurt her just by touching her. I didn't
know exactly where the disease pained her.

Mom said, "Why don't you tell Grandma about what happened
at school yesterday with the Kool-Aid?"

"But that's a dumb story," I said.

"Okay, I'll tell it," Mom said. "One of Jeremy's classmates had a
birthday party at school yesterday, and Jeremy and his friend Jennifer
were assigned—"

"It wasn't Jennifer," I corrected. "It was Shana."

"Why don't you go on and tell it?" Mom said.

Grandma squeezed my hand and said, "I'd like to hear you tell it."

"We were assigned to make a pitcher of Kool-Aid," I said. "But
when everyone drank the Kool-Aid it was too sweet—like syrup."
Grandma laughed a little. "So we looked at the packet and realized
we'd misread the directions and put in about four times more sugar
than we were supposed to."

Grandma laughed a little—softly, briefly—and that was it, that
was basically all the time I spent beside her. We left soon and walked
down the long, quiet hallway to our car. Outside, it was a cold dusk.
We drove into Sedalia, following Grandpa's car, and pulled into a
buffet steak house to eat dinner. Kent, Lucretia, Brad, and Melissa

joined us. They'd flown in yesterday and had visited with Grandma both yesterday and today. It was good to see them. Here was my family. But it was not a fun time. It was not the usual kind of gathering. We ate, we talked. I looked forward to dessert, but the prospect of all-you-can-eat sweets was largely ruined by the fact that the soft-serve ice cream machine was broken. I ate what I could, which was too much, and the car ride home seemed long, and only after I got home—while brushing my teeth—did I realize I hadn't even noticed Grandma's wig. It had been a good enough wig that it looked like business as usual.

Guard

April, sweet and cruel.

Rounded clouds, clear water. A gathering fullness. Last week came the wild geraniums, sweet rocket, lily of the valley. Dogwood blooms shining on the hillside. Blackhaw still out, and mayapples, and columbine. Some oak leaves are still pink. This week, the irises. Blooms are a way of telling time.

The white cat crosses the far pasture. The seeds of the maple tree spin down. The grass of April seems counterfeit compared to the grass of May. Well, I heard something; I thought it was an owl. Careful, careful. Is that flint? About half a mile. Someday. Straight north.

Thunder, and Teddy runs from the front porch into the yard, barking. He runs all the way to the driveway, then the thunder subsides, and he returns, little dog, to the porch again, and waits, listening. None of his people are home. His little black cat is not around.

The thunder comes again, and he charges into the yard, chasing the thunder—barking, barking—chasing it to the driveway. Get out of here! This is me telling you! Stay on that side of the driveway! This is me telling you! This is me!

The rumbling slowly fades, retreats back into the sky, and Teddy stands in the yard, still barking at it, his feet planted firmly, holding his ground. Then he trots to the porch again, but before he reaches

it, the thunder returns, and he turns and dashes toward the driveway again, barking. He barks, pivoting in a circle, until the thunder
is gone, then he barks a bit longer. It has not rained. He walks to the
porch. He sits there, waiting.

We Are Weak

On the last Sunday of April, 1984, the Missouri House of Representatives was still in session, and that's the reason Dad did not visit Grandma that day, as he had every other Sunday that month. The legislative session was the busiest time of year for Dad's office, and as the session wore on, each day was busier than the one before—complexities piled upon complexities, urgencies crowded by urgencies—until finally the gavel came down at midnight on the last day, and the legislators threw their stacks of bills into the air, and that was the end of that. The Sunday afternoon session had been harried, and Dad and his staff of legislative analysts were spread thin—fielding queries, redrafting bills, monitoring activity on the floor of the House, working with the chief clerk to keep everything running smoothly, conferring with the speaker on procedural points—and tomorrow would only be worse, and longer, since it was the last day of the session. Whatever bills did not come up for a vote tomorrow would not have another chance at life for many months.

Dad arrived home after seven Sunday evening and Mom warmed up a plate of dinner for him and he was just sitting down when the phone rang. Mom answered it, and Dad put down his knife and fork—not yet having taken a bite of food—intuiting that the call was for him. He expected that it was someone from work, but when Mom handed the phone over to him—her palm cupped over the mouthpiece—she said, "Doctor Allcorn."

Between the moment Mom spoke the doctor's name and when Dad took the receiver and said hello, there was just enough time to realign his state of mind from work and the present, to his family and his past, and then to his family and the present.

"Hello," he said.

"Darrell. It's Don Allcorn."

"Hello, Don."

"I'm sorry to interrupt your evening, but I wanted to call sooner rather than later."

Dad and Don had been roommates for a semester in college, in 1959, and because of that, and also because Don was one of the nicest men he knew, there was an honesty and ease in the way they communicated that was not at all akin to the businesslike interactions he'd had with Grandma's other doctors. Doctor Allcorn had been in charge of Grandma's care since she moved to Sedalia, and he was the one who had ordered her transfer from the nursing home to the local hospital early in the month when her white blood cell count had dropped so low, and he was the one who had discussed code blues with Dad, and he was the one, four days ago, who had advised Dad and Grandpa, in carefully phrased language, that it was the right thing to do to cease the chemotherapy. Now here was Don, calling from home on his own time, saying that he'd seen Grandma this morning, and that he'd checked in with the nurses just a few minutes ago, and that the situation was evolving, and that if at all possible, Dad should come tomorrow. He spoke specifically about a few of the issues at hand, and then asked if he should call Grandpa, and Dad said no, he'd talk to him, but then he instantly changed his mind, and said, yes, he would appreciate that.

After he hung up, Dad spoke to Mom briefly, and then he went and got the list of his staff's home phone numbers, and the first call he made was to his assistant director—he laid out what needed to be done tomorrow, how certain complications should be handled, which assignments to give which staff members—and he was on the phone off and on for the next hour and a half, and in between calls, he ate.

In the morning, in the car, Dad's mind was of two parts. On the one hand, there was a gathering clarity, a sense of purpose. Everything was drawing itself toward a single point, and that point was near, and everything outside of that point was essentially irrelevant. But on the other hand there was the narrative of the past several months, which he played and replayed, shifting it backward and forward, unsteadily, restlessly, as if from this tangle there was a way he could construct a sense of meaning or explanation or peace or even— somehow—escape. It was in his character to do this, to aim for a mastery of the details. But this search was fruitless, and tiring, and there was no single day or moment or thought or feeling or bit of bad weather or difficult conversation or view of dawn or smell of illness or bad night's sleep that occupied his mind for more than a split second. Finally, though, he came to April and settled into it, running through the month over and over. He remembered the first week—Elizabeth winning the speech contest, Elizabeth getting into Carleton College, then, on Friday, Grandma being moved to the Sedalia hospital. Temporarily, they'd thought. He had not been there the day she was moved, even though he'd taken the day off. That morning, he'd cleaned up the limbs from a silver maple he'd had trimmed; after that he took two steers to the market ($768.23); and finally he went to Elizabeth and Susan's track meet at Eldon. It had been a dizzying spring day with high, fast clouds. Elizabeth won the high jump and took second in the 800; the 1600-meter relay team of E. Jackson, S. Jackson, Olsen, and Bryant took second, too. It was Susan's first high school track medal. Then two days later, when he made his Sunday visit to Grandma—the first time he'd seen her in the Sedalia hospital—he had to wear a hospital gown and booties and a mask because they were worried about her getting an infection, and his spring hay fever had been giving him fits, and wearing the mask just made him miserable with the sneezing and running nose. Then . . . the next week. He bought fifty-three bales of timothy hay from Junior Goldammer ($106.00). They were fantastic hay bales— heavy, tight, rich with scent. That was also the week the floor refinish-ers came ($277.00). After they left, and the floors were safe to walk on, their shine gave him the impression of walking on glass. That weekend, they bought two new chairs for the living room ($502.52) and a new color TV ($524.57). Then came the Osage track meet, the Versailles track meet, the Warrensburg relays. Also, the blood clot in Grandma's leg—the swelling, the discomfort. The way her abdomen was swollen, too, her liver wracked by the disease. She was as discouraged as she'd ever been. The Sunday visit when her feeding tube became blocked for half an hour before it mysteriously started running again, no thanks to the nurses who'd fretted with it. Watching her sleep—or, well, doze—and how her hands fluttered—more active than when she was awake—and how she talked incomprehensibly in her sleep, and he couldn't help but listen for meaning, but really there was none, unless the meaning was this: when we are weak, words bubble up on their own. (She had said, "It can go." She had said, "Rope.") On Good Friday—the day Elizabeth flew to visit Cornell—Aunt Billie called him at work to say that Clarice had gone into Windsor Hospital with pneumonia. Apparently, when Clarice had called that morning to tell Billie she was going to the hospital, Billie didn't recognize her sister's voice because it was so hoarse; she'd had to ask who was calling. On Easter Sunday, Elizabeth had returned from Cornell, more or less glowing with excitement, and announced while setting the dinner table that she finally knew for sure where she wanted to go to college. The next day, Monday, a week ago, had been Clarice's seventy-ninth birthday—she was still in the hospital—and also the thirty-sixth anniversary of the day Grandma and Grandpa had moved the family from Kansas City to the farm. There was the track meet at Helias, the relays at Osage Beach, the dwindling days of the legislative session—each day like a parody of the one before, getting home at eight o'clock, or nine, or after ten. Friday, he wrote a check to Cornell, a deposit of two hundred dollars.

When Dad got to her room, there was no one else there. She was on her side, in the fetal position, and he could tell that she'd lost several more pounds just in the last week. She was not asleep, she was unconscious, and it was the first time he'd seen her like that, the first time he was unable to greet her, tell her *I'm here*. She wasn't moving except for shallow breaths. He sat and rubbed her shoulder and back. He pushed her hair out of her face. Soon, Grandpa came, and they both sat there, and the nurses spoke with them, then Doctor Allcorn came by and they went into the hallway to talk, then they sat with her again, but there was no difference between the way she looked now and the way she'd looked when he had arrived. Soon, Dad heard his stomach growling, and he and Grandpa decided to go get something to eat. It was nearly noon. He hadn't eaten much for breakfast. He was wearing a suit because he planned to drive straight to work after the visit, and he and Grandpa took the elevator down to the cafeteria and they bought their food—had to wait in line a few minutes—and had sat down and were starting to eat when Dad saw one of Grandma's nurses across the room, and she was look-ing for someone, scanning the dining room, and when she saw Dad, he realized she was looking for him, and she started walking in his direction, and Dad said to Grandpa, "The nurse," and Grandpa turned around to see her, and she reached their table and said that they should come back upstairs, so they did, left their food there, fol-lowed her, rode the elevator, didn't talk, and they got up to the room and another nurse was in there, standing there, and she moved aside, and Grandpa went to the bedside, and Dad came beside him, then Doctor Allcorn appeared again, and also another nurse, and Doctor Allcorn spoke, and wrote on her chart, and he then led them, all of them, in a prayer, then it was a moment when everyone suddenly had a task to do, including Dad and Grandpa, and their task was to be in the room with her, alone, for a brief time, and after that they went into the hallway and spoke with Doctor Allcorn some more, and then Dad saw Uncle Emmett, Grandma's only sibling, coming down the hallway, and Emmett said he'd just been down in the cafe-teria looking for them, and Dad told him the news and Emmett nodded and said, "I was up here at noon. I thought she was sleeping." Dad and Emmett went into her room. After a minute, Dad left him there, and he went to the nurses' station and he called home and told Mom and asked her to make a couple of phone calls for him, and then he hung up and called Kent, and while he was on the phone with Kent, Grandpa came beside him, and so he handed the phone over to Grandpa for a little bit, and then they hung up and Grandpa got out his little pocket notebook and opened it and there was written the number for the Windsor funeral home.

Mom called Dad's office, spoke to his secretary and his assistant director. She hung up and called the school, and spoke to the secretary and the principal. The secretary looked up Elizabeth's class schedule. It was just after lunch for the high schoolers; they'd been in fifth period only a few minutes, and that meant that Elizabeth was just down the hallway in Mrs. Engelbrecht's room, so the secretary got up and went out of the office and around the corner and knocked on Mrs. Engelbrecht's door. She spoke to Mrs. Engelbrecht and Mrs. Engelbrecht called Elizabeth up to her desk and Elizabeth came and then followed the secretary back to the office and the secretary handed her the phone. Mom was on the line and she spoke to Elizabeth. Mom also wanted to talk to Susan, so the secretary was looking up her class schedule. The secretary asked Elizabeth if she knew where my classroom was, and she said yes, and so she went into the hallway and gathered a couple of things from her locker and put on her jacket, and then went back past the principal's office and turned like she was going to the cafeteria. She came to Mrs. Davis's room.

We were reading silently, and there was a knock on the door, and through the narrow slit of a window in the door, I recognized the jean jacket. The door opened, and there was my sister, and I knew.

Her Existing Sixteen Journal Entries from April 30 Turned into One Journal Entry

The math: $(1968 + 1969 + 1970 + 1971 + 1972 + 1973 + 1974 + 1975 + 1976 + 1977 + 1978 + 1979 + 1980 + 1981 + 1982 + 1983) \div 16 = 1975.5$

April 30, 1975.5

Heard it rain a little in the nite and then we have had a good shower this morning. Got up at 5:50 a.m. again—a beautiful day—beautiful day. Baked a cake, cooked for today & tomorrow. Belford had a new calf this morning. Beautiful day—hair done. I set out cabbage, tomato & onion sets & planted flowers. Belford watched the ball game. I took a nap. Fixed a salad & deviled eggs to take to Warrensburg today to Johnson County Extension Spring Event. It's been a beautiful day. Had a note from Lucretia today letting us know Bradley has a job this summer to work on computer for a medical company. I baked a peach cobbler—went to town.

 Fair in afternoon—cleaned cabinet woodwork—baked cherry pie & made crusts—Freda took piano lesson. Another beautiful day and warmer. We planted more green beans, three rows sweet corn & flowers. Cleaning part of kitchen cabinets—finished cleaning them at 2:45 in the afternoon. I've baked a cake—made pie filling. Has been very nice day— house cleaned the north room upstairs today. Belford has gone to Sedalia to get the tractor radiator he took yesterday afternoon. Belford went to sale & took a cow and two calves. Rested this afternoon and read. Belford

went to Kansas City today with 20 calves he sold, got home 2:30. I house
cleaned the living room today and early in morning baked a coffee cake
and loaf of banana bread. Also baked a lemon pie & made a meat loaf.
Busy busy.

A cloudy cool day. Has been cloudy all day but we had no rain.
Belford had electrical work done all morning in house so I couldn't do
much. Cloudy all day, very light rain by 3:00 p.m. We moved cows home
this morning. Gerald & Everett helped. We had a total of 1.2 inches rain
& it came wonderful—slow & easy. Went down to Lulu's awhile to see her
new kitchen carpet in late afternoon. Chilly all day and windy. There was
a bad tornado in south part of Springfield last night. Has been cloudy &
had some light showers all day but I got the dining room curtains washed
& dried. Has rained all day—2½ inches by nite.

A dark dismal rainy day and still raining—has rained all day.
Chilly all day and windy. Sewing club at Hazel's tonite. We went to
church at nite. Church at nite. A great service tonite. Tonite was Patriotic
nite. Really cool tonite. Home in evening.

Home at nite. Home at nite. Home at nite.

Houston's Creek

Thirty-two years earlier, April 30, 1952, Darrell and Kent finished lunch—eating as fast as they could without getting scolded—grabbed their fishing poles and two tin cans, and ran into the pasture. Past the weep spring, Darrell came to a place where there were dozens of old, dried-up cow pies. "Over here!" he cried to Kent, who was looking for cow pies over by the fenceline. The two of them kicked over the cow pies and collected worms.

It was a sunny day that felt particularly good because just a week ago school had let out for the summer, and therefore the possibilities of the season loomed large and radiant. Darrell and Kent had gone fishing every day since the end of school. Now, as the brothers walked across the rest of the north pasture, Darrell decided he would continue to fish every day, weather permitting, until the ponds and creeks got low and doggy in July.

They climbed the fence—which meant they were leaving the farm—walked down the High Line Railroad for a bit, then followed Houston's Creek downstream until they came to what they called the first pool. There, they put worms on their hooks and approached the water. Darrell walked to the far end, where the water was deepest. The little *plop* the worm made as it hit the water was a wonderful sound.

By the time the creek passed beneath the blacktop, Darrell had caught two little perch—and let them go—and Kent had caught one. Past the blacktop, the creek turned west and grew larger. It held more potential. They splashed through some shallows, cut through

a thicket, then came back down to the water by one of Darrell's favorite holes. It was a glossy stretch of water within a deep bower of
shade. They had no luck there, but picked up and went to the next
hole—which they called "flat rock hole" because of an outcropping
of limestone—and here Kent caught a nice perch and Darrell was
watching his brother hold up his catch when he noticed his own cork
bobber nudge sideways a little bit, then nudge again, and then go
under. It was a catfish for sure, because they were always slow and
nibbly about the bait. He pulled his rod back and felt the fish—it was
big—and the whole world collapsed to include nothing other than
him, the fish, and the taut line between them. He felt his blood rising, and an approaching joy, and then suddenly the line went loose
and the fish was gone and he said, "No!"

"You had one?" Kent called from the other end of the pool.

"A big one! He got away. I'm sure it was a catfish."

Darrell sat down, and he inspected his line and his hook. The
worm was gone. His heartbeat was audible. He was disappointed.
For a while, he just sat and watched Kent fish. He listened to a
red-winged blackbird nearby. *Chek . . . chek . . . cora-lee!* He took
off his cap and wiped his brow with his handkerchief and put
his hat back on. Finally he put on a new worm and fished again,
though he knew that he'd missed his chance with this hole. But
the thing about Houston's Creek was that around each bend there
was a new fishing hole, and each one was different—looked different, smelled different, held different fish. The creek was a string
of unique worlds that went all the way to another creek, and then
that creek went to the Blackwater River, and the Blackwater River
went all the way to the Missouri, and the Missouri trudged to the
Mississippi, and the Mississippi lumbered to the Gulf of Mexico,
and that was the ocean. Darrell liked to think about that. But anyway, if one fishing hole didn't work out, all you had to do was walk
to the next one, and so on and so forth, working your way through
Mr. Houston's farm, or even beyond, until you got tired or satisfied
or ran out of daylight or worms. Or just decided that you didn't
want the walk home to get any longer than it already was.

They weren't yet done today, though, so they walked up the bank and through a small pasture and then back down to the water.

Instead of following the creek home, Darrell and Kent cut overland, making a shorter trip of it, though admittedly a hotter one, and when they reached the farm again, they felt the happiness of return, even though the farmhouse was still far away. They were tired, and hadn't spoken in a long while, and Darrell started thinking about how his father had taught him to fish just four years ago, as soon as they'd moved to the farm. And he thought about how much he'd learned about fishing since then, and how much more he would know four years from now, and he thought about how next year would be his last year at Sunnyside School, and after that he'd go to high school in Windsor. By the time it happened, he decided, he would be ready for it.

They reached the house, and Darrell called for Mother through the screen door. There was no answer. They walked around the corner of the house, and there she was, taking down wash from the clothesline.

"Look," Darrell said, holding up his catch.

"Now there's a fine fish," Mother said. "And look at Kent's, too."

Yes, their creek was connected to all the oceans of the world, and that was a grand thing, and it was an adventure to follow it, and someday follow farther, and someday see the ocean, and someday be a man, but all of that—everything that lay in front of Darrell, all the promise, all the hope—didn't mean anything at all, didn't matter one whit, without Mother there to return to. She was his home. She was his beginning.

He admired his fish. He said, "We had a good day."

The God of Mildred Jackson

A decision had been made not to crowd the farmhouse with grand-kids, and so from the parking lot of the funeral home, after the visitation ended, and after the adults were done talking, Elizabeth, Susan, Melissa, and I followed Jim and Linda's car out into the countryside, through the darkness, to their house. It was late. When we arrived we all came inside and Linda took us down into the basement and showed us our beds. The basement seemed about as big as our whole house. It had a couple of bedrooms, where the girls would sleep, a bathroom, a kitchen, and one long, big living room. In the open space of the big room was a couch. That was my bed, where I now lay in the dark.

It was not a bad bed. Linda had tucked a sheet around the couch cushions, then put a sheet and blanket on top of that. It was as homey as a bed on a couch could be. There was a dense silence in the basement, a solid darkness. I'd never spent the night at Jim and Linda's house—none of us had. For a time, I had listened to the sounds of my sisters and cousin getting ready for bed—running water, muffled talk. But they'd been in bed for several minutes now, and were quiet.

I thought of school. What did people think about me being away because my grandma had died? I remembered walking out of the school in the early afternoon, two days ago, with Elizabeth—walking down the long hall, everything hushed, the classroom doors closed. I was carrying my notebook and my jacket. We walked out of the school and into the parking lot, the gravel crunching beneath our feet. I saw the truck, and Susan was waiting there, and the sun was high. We drove away. School would go on without us.

I had sat with Teddy that night, at the end of the sidewalk. I told him about Grandma. When it got dark, I went inside. Later, I came back out and looked for Teddy. I couldn't find him. I walked around the house to the front porch. I kneeled and looked in his house. There he was. I said his name, and he woke up and looked at me.

"Are you okay?" I asked him.

At the visitation tonight in the funeral home, Grandma had looked better than when I'd seen her in March. Her hair was right. Her lipstick, too. She was Grandma. I had stood there with Mom and Susan, and later with Dad and Grandpa. She was only a few feet away from me, just below eye level, and the lighting was warm and diffuse, and the stillness was total. She looked good. She was Grandma. (I was I.) Still, the question of what I was supposed to think about was a difficult one, even with Mom beside me saying didn't she look peaceful, and that she had loved us very much, and that now she wasn't in pain anymore. What thoughts should I formulate?

A little earlier, I had stood by my mother while she spoke with the funeral director's wife.

"In all the years of being in the choir, and singing in the quartet with her, and socializing with her," this woman said, "I never once knew her to hit a sour note, not as an organist and not as a person. And earlier today, I want to tell you, I was in here vacuuming and cleaning the room for tonight, and she was already in here, you know, though the casket was closed, and I want to tell you that as I cleaned, I sang. I sang to her."

This was not the funeral. The funeral was tomorrow. This was the visitation. People came and went, they spoke to Grandpa, to Dad, to Kent, to Mom, to Lucretia. Lots of people knew who I was, but I didn't know who they were. They were old people, like Grandma and Grandpa. They were Grandma and Grandpa's friends, and they knew my name, had seen pictures of me in my Little League uniform, or playing with my sisters in a pile of October leaves. Or I had once fallen asleep in their arms when I was just a wee little thing. I had been in their house long ago, I probably didn't remember, I had spilled juice. I had eaten cake. I had whistled a tune for them. I was about the age of their grandson. I had so much hair. Grandma was a special lady. (I was I.) People cried, but quietly. The steps outside the funeral home were lit. A flagpole was near. Susan was standing with me. We were just standing. The stars were out. We had asked if we could go outside for a little bit and Mom said okay. Susan looked at the flagpole and said, "Remember how Wayne climbed the flagpole at the swimming pool?"

Dark carpeting. Clean hands.

Suddenly, there was screaming.

There was screaming—loud screaming—and darkness, and they left no room for anything else. And then I remembered myself, and I was startled by the screaming, scared because it seemed so close, and I sat up in the darkness, the total darkness, and I realized the screaming was me. It was in me, it was from me, it was around me. It came from someplace so deep inside me that I hadn't recognized it at first. The screaming didn't seem like something I would do, but I was doing it, and I heard voices, and a light flicked on nearby—"Jeremy!"—and then the light in the room came on, and Elizabeth was there and she said "Jeremy!" again. She came over. I had stopped screaming. Susan and Melissa were looking at me from the door to their bedroom.

"What's wrong?" Elizabeth asked.

I said, "I didn't know where I was."

"Everything's okay," she said. "We're at Jim and Linda's house."

I nodded. "I know."

"Do you want a drink of water?" she asked.

"No."

"Well . . . ," she said. "How about let's leave a light on? It's dark down here."

We left the bathroom light on, with the bathroom door partly closed, and the girls went back into their rooms, and I heard them getting into their beds, and I got back under my covers, which had been thrown into disarray by my outburst. I felt embarrassed because of the screaming. We'd been in bed only fifteen minutes or so. I didn't know what had happened to me. I didn't understand it. I hadn't done it on purpose. It had come from somewhere inside. I didn't know: maybe it was still there.

In another basement, the church basement, we ate lunch the next day. It was the meal for our family before the funeral, but among the dozens of diners, I recognized only maybe one out of four people. I wasn't hungry. My neck was tight in my dress shirt. There was a line for the food, but we didn't have to wait in it. People stepped aside, told us to please go ahead.

It was cloudy and dim outside, and maybe it would rain, and maybe it would get even windier, and we climbed the stairs out of the basement and stood in the foyer and people looked at us again— people coming in—and Dad talked to many people, and Mom stayed with me and Susan and Elizabeth, and a woman told her what a fine-looking family we were. The people moving into the church were moving slowly. It was full in there. You could tell without even looking. It was a big church, and it was full.

We went in—Susan, Elizabeth, Mom, Lucretia, Brad, Melissa, and I—with a deacon leading us. We went down the aisle. The pews were full. The deacon stopped at the second pew from the front and asked Mom if this was enough room, if we would fit, and she said yes, so we filed in. We sat. I was between Susan and Mom. Mom was the last in, and she realized she'd miscounted by one— that there wasn't quite enough room. She perched at the end of the pew, scrunched up against me. I moved over as much as I could. We all nudged over a little. Mom settled back, but she had barely enough seat. She perched there. She looked to the front of the church, where Grandma lay. Just now, Grandpa, Dad, and Kent were coming down the aisle, passing Mom. They went to Grandma. Mom thought to herself, I can do this. I can sit here. I can make it.

We watched. Dad, Grandpa, Kent. The casket was surrounded by a slope of flowers. Grandpa put his hands on the edge of the casket. He bent down and kissed Grandma on the cheek. Beside me, Susan cried. In front, Dad wiped his eyes. Grandpa stepped back. The three men stood there in their suits. They linked arms. The organ music continued. The church was full, so full. I looked over at the organ. There was some lady playing the organ. Then I realized it was the funeral director's wife, the one who told Mom last night how she'd sung to Grandma.

The men were sitting down. They were in front of us. Emmett was there, too, and Clarice and Billie.

Soon, the organ music ended. Some people in the audience cleared their throats. In front of us, Aunt Clarice coughed. She'd left the hospital just for the funeral, even though the doctors thought her pneumonia was still too serious for her to go anywhere.

The pastor stood up from his chair and came to the pulpit.

He said, slowly, "From the hand of the apostle Paul, in his second letter to the church at Corinth, we read: 'Blessed be the God and Father of our Lord, Jesus Christ, the father of mercies and God of all comfort, who comforts us in all our affliction, so that we may be able to comfort those who are in any affliction, with the comfort with which we ourselves are comforted by God.'"

The pastor sat down. Behind him, the choir stood up. They were in their white robes. At a nod from the choir leader, the piano and organ started up together. The choir came in, voices rising, voices together—men and women, melody and harmony. There were words. There was "Jerusalem." There was "Hosanna." There was an old temple and a shadow of a cross. The song swelled, ebbed, swelled again, then again, and the voices came to an end, the piano returned to silence, and for a while the organ went on, chords so strong that they were felt within your chest, then that, too, ended, and then there was the memory of the music, the imprint it had left, like how a flashbulb makes an image on your retina. Soon that, too, faded, and we remembered silence, and non-music.

The choir sat down, making a certain rustling sound with their robes.

After a moment, the man sitting beside the pastor—an older

man, another pastor?—stood and came to the pulpit. He arranged his Bible, his notes. He looked out at us, then down to his reading.

He said, "The writer of Proverbs says, 'The good wife has a statute of honor. She is more precious than jewels. Trusted by her husband, wise, industrious in providing for the needs of her household, even to the point of engaging in commerce, considerate of the less fortunate, and praised by all her family.'"

His voice was lower than the first man's. It was slower. It was sadder. It was a country voice.

"And the Psalmist wrote, 'The Lord is my shepherd, I shall not want. He makes me lie down in green pastures. He leads me beside still waters. He restores my soul. He leads me in paths of righteousness, for his namesake. Even though I walk through the valley of the shadow of death, I will fear no evil, for thou art with me, thy rod and thy staff, they comfort me. Thou preparest a table before me in the presence of mine enemies. Thou annointest my head with oil, my cup overflows. Surely goodness and mercy shall follow me all the days of my life. And I will dwell in the house of the Lord forever.'

"And the apostle John in the fourteenth chapter of his gospel: '"In my father's house are many rooms, if it were not so, I would have told you. Would I have told you that I go to prepare a place for you? And when I go and prepare a place for you, I will come again and will take you to myself that where I am you may be also. And you know the way where I am going." Thomas said to him, "Lord, we do not know where you are going. And how can we know the way?" Jesus said to him, "I am the way, the truth and the life, no one comes to the Father but by me. If you had known me, you would have known my Father also. Henceforth, you know him, and have seen him. I will not leave you comfortless. I will come to you. Peace I leave with you. My peace I give to you. Let not your hearts be troubled, neither let them be afraid."'

"Let us pray: Our Father in heaven, we thank you so much for these words of comfort and assurance and hope from the scripture. Our Father, we thank you for the precious promises of this book on which we build our lives and in which we trust. Father, we thank you especially today for the life of Mildred Jackson. We thank you, Father, for every good thing that you brought into this world through her life. We thank you for every contribution that she made to us. We thank you for every gift to her husband and family, to her church, to all who knew her. Our Father, we thank you for the richness that has come to our lives because we have touched her life. And Father, we thank you that in your love and your mercy that you have taken her from illness to be with you in that home where there is no sickness, no death, no separation. And Father, we thank you most of all today for your son, Jesus Christ, who loved us and gave himself for us, that we might come to this hour and sorrow not, as those who have no hope. We thank you, Father, that Jesus has changed this hour to an hour of triumph, when we can celebrate together the passing of our loved one into that life that is eternal. Father, we pray now that as we wait before you, you will give us the presence of your Holy Spirit—the great comforter—to speak peace to our hearts and courage. And we pray, in the name of our Lord, Jesus Christ. Amen."

Even as he sat down, the organ started again, and one choir member—a woman—stepped up front. Her voice came to us alone, and sang a song called "Victory in Jesus." It was a proud song, and sure, and lasted just the right length of time.

When the singer returned to her seat, the young preacher came to the pulpit again.

"Reading again from the hand of Paul, in his first letter to the church at Corinth, in the fifteenth chapter, we read these words: 'When the perishable puts on the imperishable, and the mortal puts on immortality, then shall come to pass the saying that is written: "Death is swallowed up in victory." "O death, where is thy victory? O death, where is thy sting?" The sting of death is sin and the power of sin is the law, but thanks be to God who gives us the victory through our Lord, Jesus Christ.'"

The preacher paused. He looked up toward the ceiling, then out into the assembly.

"The victory through our Lord, Jesus Christ. 'Victory in Jesus,' as Jean has just sung for us. How appropriate at such a time as this.

It's true, it's useless to try and deceive ourselves. Death is a reality. We view death as an enemy. It seems at times, as today, that death conquers and destroys. But in these moments, in the days out in the future, as we consider our loss, death only seems victorious. The reality of all that's happened in these last days doesn't seem believable. Belford has lost his wife of almost forty-nine years. Darrell and Ann and Kent and Lucretia have lost a mother. Elizabeth and Susan and Melissa and Brad and Jeremy have lost a grandmother. Emmett has lost a sister, Linda an aunt. Many other family members and a great host of friends have lost a dear friend. Death seems victorious at first glance, but his conquest isn't real. Christ has come, and death is swallowed up in victory, victory in Jesus.

"Paul reminds us that deliverance has been granted to all believers. We are free from the burdens and the losses, and the sorrows which death brings to those who don't have victory in Jesus. We are victorious over these things of death. They're replaced by freedom, and forgiveness, and eternal joy. 'O grave, where is your victory? Death, where is your sting?' Death waves a banner, he tries to terrorize all of us who pass his way. He leads a host of banner wavers, but death has no prints of nails in his hands, or his feet. There is no victory for death—Jesus has passed through his territory. Jesus has torn down the banners of death, he's broken the gates, he's made it possible for us to pass by death unafraid. Death no longer reigns, his scepter is broken.

"Then Paul breaks into praise, an anthem. And I'm convinced this afternoon that he would call us to join in. 'Thanks be to God.' 'Thanks be to God,' he says—what a strange song to sing at such a time. And yet, it's not so strange. 'Thanks be to God.' Thanks be to God for the seventy-plus years he gave to Mildred. Thanks be to God for all the joys that she shared with her husband and her family and her friends. Thanks be to God for her sweet, sweet spirit in all things toward all people. Thanks be to God for her tremendous abilities and her musical gifts and her willingness to always share them with those about her. Thanks be to God for Mildred's loving spirit. Thanks be to God for her example. Thanks be to God for her patience, even in her suffering. Thanks be to God for her uncomplaining spirit. Thanks be to God that Mildred had known our savior for many years. Thanks be to God," he choked up, paused, then continued in a croak, "the victory is hers."

"Let's bow for prayer."

It was a long silence. Then:

"Father, we come to you this afternoon grateful, thankful for Mildred, thankful, Father, that in so many ways she's touched our lives. Thankful, Father, that she's gone from this life to a better place. Thankful that one who loved her, far beyond the loves that this life offers, meets all of her needs now. Father, help us to so live, help us to so respond to Christ, that when our time comes we might have victory, and that there might be glad reunion again. And Father, we ask these things in the name of he who's above every name. Amen."

The preacher stepped back from the pulpit. He picked up a book. The choir stood—that rushing noise of their robes—and suddenly, everyone was standing. The organ came in, announced the song. Paper rustled as people opened their programs to read the words. Then the voices of the entire congregation—women, men, children, preacher, deacons, choir—rose together. The great space of the chapel was filled with song. It was a sound that was unified and unifying. It was round. It was not too much; it was not too little.

(Sweetness. Something. I wondered at it.)

Amazing grace! how sweet the sound
That saved a wretch like me!
I once was lost, but now am found,
Was blind, but now I see.

'Twas grace that taught my heart to fear,
And grace my fears relieved;
How precious did that grace appear
The hour I first believed!

Thro' many dangers, toils, and snares,
I have already come;
'Tis grace hath bro't me safe thus far
And grace will lead me home.

The Lord has promised good to me,
His work my hope secures;
He will my shield and portion be
As long as life endures.

When we've been there ten thousand years,
Bright shining as the sun,
We've no less days to sing God's praise
Than when we first begun.

The song ended, the organ stopped, but the music was still present. We were all still standing. We had come through. The preacher was at the pulpit again.

He said, "May the God of Abraham, Isaac, and Jacob, and the God of Mildred Jackson, bless us and keep us, may he surround us with his strong and comforting arm, and fill us with his peace that passes all human understanding. Amen."

She was carried down the aisle by six men, and she was set in the foyer, and everyone passed her on the way out, and we came last, the family, and Mom reminded me and Susan and Elizabeth that this would be the last time we would see her, and we paused, and considered, and looked at her, then moved past her a little bit, and Uncle Emmett came to her, and he was crying, this big prairie farmer, and he said to his sister, "You're with Mother and Daddy now."

Out. Out in the day. Out in the sun. The sun! The early afternoon sunlight of spring, dazzling our eyes, still a bit of wind, the warmth of the sunlight on our faces, the steps of the church covered with green plastic carpeting, and the crowds of people still there, and

Susan and Elizabeth both crying, and then the casket comes out of the church, and down the stairs, and into the hearse, the car's back gate closes, and we walk to our own car, and get in, and it is warm inside—heated by the sun—and Susan is still crying, I am not, and it is otherwise quiet in the car. Dad is with Grandpa and Kent in another car, Mom drives us, we queue up, we wait, then the line of cars is moving through the streets of Windsor, everyone stops and pulls over for us, we ignore stop signs, we are like a train—all these cars, linked together—and on the edge of town, in the cemetery, we stop.

Afterward, there is a feeling of ease. There is nothing left to do. Grandpa continues to receive condolences. The funeral director speaks with him about a couple of details. Then, all of a sudden, there is no one in front of Grandpa. He sees the sunlight. He looks around. There, just across the road from the family plot, is the farm where he grew up—the pasture where he raced ponies with his friends.

We drove home that night, all five of us. Susan had dress rehearsal for a dance recital tomorrow. I had the elementary track meet. We all had school. We'd missed three and a half days already.

In the car, I thought. I chewed gum and thought. For so long, we'd been living with Grandma's illness, not knowing for sure where it was headed or when, and all that time we'd been anticipating her death, seeing it get closer, seeing that it was coming. I'd carried that with me: *Grandma will die.* That's what we'd all carried, that was the nugget of dread that had been with us through the winter and spring. But now *Grandma will die* was no longer true; she suddenly, instantly, wasn't going to die anymore, because she already had died, and it was necessary to replace the months-long anticipation of her death with something new, and to do it quickly, to keep up with what was actually happening. I had expected a monumental wave of sadness to come over me, but it didn't. Perhaps I had fought it too strongly. I had been afraid of it. I had not wanted to cry at the funeral, and I had succeeded. Besides, I already felt sadness. Sadness had been with me before she had died. But now that she was gone, wasn't there supposed to be a change, a sort of *click: this is how to feel now, this is the right way, this is okay.* There was no click. There was just me. And inside me was the sadness, yes, but nestled in alongside the sadness was another thing: a not-feeling. It was not anger. It was not fear. It was not despair. It was a not-feeling. So that was the only thing that was new since Grandma had died.

I could add things up. I could count days. I could imagine pain. I could think about myself, wonder about others. At the moment there was a certain calm. Meanwhile, it was spring. Meanwhile, answers were elusive. Thought applied to thought produced more thought. I was eleven years old. I had blond hair. I had a mother and father, who each had a mother and father, who each had a mother and father, and so on.

How hard was I supposed to try?

Then

Then, after a little bit, Daddy said Mildred's name and came walking from the direction of the house. She couldn't see his face, but she could see the outline of his head—the tilt of it—and that was enough. He carried her home, and she could hear Trixie following them, and she didn't know how Daddy could see in the dark, but he could.

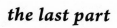

the last part

Normally, We Got Normal Milk

The playground was set above the black cinder track. At the far end of the playground, the lunch ladies had set up long tables outside the big shed where the buses were worked on. There stood all the usual lunch ladies wearing the same aprons and hairnets, looking happier than usual in the daylight, and the tables in front of them were loaded with white paper sacks. You went up, grabbed a sack lunch, grabbed a carton of chocolate milk, and that was it. Inside the bag was a cold-cut sandwich, a bag of potato chips, three carrot sticks, an apple, a napkin, a packet of mustard, and a packet of mayonnaise. Except for the last day of school, this was the only day of the year we got sack lunches. It was also the only time we got chocolate milk. Normally, we got normal milk. In addition, as if the food and presentation weren't wonderful enough already, each sack also contained a little Styrofoam cup of vanilla ice cream. When you were done with your first stuff (or not), you peeled back the paper lid on the ice cream, and dug in with a small wooden spoon that was basically a thumb-sized tongue depressor. By the time you got to your ice cream it had started to go slightly soft. In other words, perfect.

That was the sack lunch.

Meanwhile, buses from five other country schools showed up and spilled all their fourth, fifth, and sixth graders out onto our playground. It was odd seeing a bunch of strangers mobbing our swingsets and our giant slide and our splinter-happy teeter-totters. These outsiders, who we had been reminded were our guests, brought their own lunches, and each school—each big clot of kids—staked out a bit of territory on the grassy slope above the track and unpacked their meals and ate.

It was a beautiful day. Gorgeous, sunny, early May perfection.

Our principal wielded a bullhorn. He went to the middle of the track and told us that the time for lunch was ending. Instead of a suit, he was wearing a short-sleeved shirt and a blue Russellville baseball cap. He had a starter's pistol in his back pocket. He welcomed all the schools and said that we sure had a nice day for a track meet, didn't we? We cheered. There must have been four hundred of us. It was as if our anthill had been unearthed and now we were swarming the playground, frantic; that's how many of us there were.

When the baton was handed to me for the lest leg of the 240-yard relay, we were behind by two strides, but I dug deep and gained on the other kid, and when we were reaching the finish line, I pushed out my chest to try and break the tape first, but we lost by a few inches. We would have to be content with second place. It was disappointing, though, and I was frustrated by my inability to overcome the gap.

The high jump started soon after that. Russellville had one high jump landing pit. Unlike the rectangular, oversized sponge things that other schools had, our landing pad was a huge bag of netting filled with hundreds of oddly shaped pieces of green foam. It was not the prettiest thing, but it did break your fall. Woe to you, though, if you dropped some loose change in it. We also had only one high jump bar. It was an aluminum bar that was bent, broken, and spliced with fabric tape. It sagged about three inches in the middle, so you had to aim your jump at just the right place or you were actually attempting a higher height than necessary. Also, where the bar had been spliced together with white tape, it was twice its usual thickness, and therefore it was in your best interest to avoid landing on top of the bar. Finally, two little tail ends of tape always hung down from the bar about four inches, and though they were not pretty, they let you know the direction and velocity of the wind.

The hooligans from the other schools didn't know how to jump. Some of them dove over the bar headfirst, which shouldn't have even

been allowed. Some of them tried to hurdle it. It was a woeful display. Only two other kids seemed to know how to flop over the bar
the right way. Even though I hadn't jumped in almost a year—since
the Junior Olympics last summer—I cleared the opening height
of three feet (ha!) and knew I was just as good as ever.

Everyone but me was out of the competition at three feet four.
The high jump official, who was a high schooler, called me over.
"That's it, you've got first."

"I want to keep jumping," I said.

"We can do that," the high schooler said.

By this point, Dad had shown up, and he and I talked a little,
and then he started taking pictures of me high jumping.

I cleared three feet six. I cleared three feet eight on my second
attempt. More people were coming over to watch. The bar went up to
three feet ten—a foot shorter than I was. It was as high as I had ever
jumped. Some of the high schoolers who were helping officiate the
meet were watching. I cleared three feet ten on the first jump. People
clapped. I rolled out of the landing pit and there was Elizabeth.

"Great jump," she said.

"If I do four feet, it's a personal record," I told her.

"You can do it," she said. "You're jumping awesome. Just remember to snap your hips up."

They moved the bar to four feet. I went back out to the front of
the pit. I had made a mark in the dirt where I started my approach.
Mr. Brumley, the ever-stern high school principal, was out there. He
was watching me with his arms crossed.

I cleared four feet on my first attempt.

The bar went to four feet two. I stood by the bar. It was as high
as my chin. I walked slowly back to my starting mark, thinking about
the jump, thinking about how to do it. I knew it was possible for me
to jump four feet two, but I also knew it was possible for me not to
jump four feet two.

On the first jump, I felt the bar brushing my back as I went over,
and after I landed in the pit I watched the bar bounce and then fall.
The crowd went, "Aww!"

On the second jump, I clipped the bar with my heels and pulled it down.

On the third jump, I approached the bar, but felt that my paces were off, and I bypassed the bar. I walked back out, started my approach again, jumped, and felt that it was a good jump—a worthy jump—but as I landed in the pit I heard the aluminum bar hit the ground. I stood up in the pit and a few people clapped. Elizabeth told me I had done great. Mr. Brumley came over and put his hand on my back and said, "Congratulations. Jumping is in your blood."

The next day, Saturday, Elizabeth high jumped five feet at the district meet in Fulton and won first place. That evening, we all met in the university auditorium in Jefferson City for Susan's dance recital. When the music for her number began, everyone was looking forward at the dimly lit stage, but then from the back of the auditorium came these sounds—hissing noises—and people started looking back there. Then we saw the dancers—Susan among them—dressed as cats, with makeup and tails and ears and leotards, hissing and clawing their way down the aisles and finally onto the stage. Then they danced.

Sunday, Dad got up early because he thought the heifer might deliver her calf today. He walked into the north pasture and looked for the heifer. She was lying underneath a cedar tree. The calf was born an hour later. It was a nice heifer calf with long ears and long legs, and we went and looked at her and Susan named her Lizzie—after Elizabeth—because the calf kept sticking its tongue out just like Elizabeth did when she was concentrating on something.

Elizabeth mailed her graduation announcements on Tuesday. Mom turned forty-four on Wednesday. Susan made her a cake. We gave her presents.

On Thursday, Wayne came over after school, and he took me, Elizabeth, and Susan down to the creek in his car. We crossed the low water bridge, then turned into the grassy parking spot above the creek—to turn around and go home. We wheeled around, slowed. I opened the door—we were all four in the front seat, and I was sitting next to the door—and at that moment Wayne gunned the engine and executed a doughnut. The door flung wide, which left me hanging on to the handle as tightly as I could. My feet were braced awkwardly inside the car, and the ground was whizzing past just a couple feet below me. Wayne saw what was happening and stopped. He explained that he hadn't seen me open the door. It wasn't exactly an apology.

Friday, Grandpa came to the state track meet. Grandpa and Mom sat in the stands and passed the binoculars back and forth. It was a hot day, and the grandstand at the university track was full. Dad was out on the field, serving as a volunteer official. Mom and Grandpa couldn't tell exactly what was going on at the high jump pit, but they could see Elizabeth jumping, clearing heights, making a few scratches here and there. They could see the field of competitors getting smaller and smaller, and the bar getting higher. There were eventually three jumpers left, and they watched them all take their three attempts at a final height, and all fail.

After a few minutes, Elizabeth walked away from the pit. They saw her talk to her coach, then to Dad. She made her way toward them. She was just on the other side of the track, but then had to wait for a heat of the hurdles before she could cross. As she was standing there, waiting, having waved to Mom and Grandpa already, they could tell she hadn't won. Then the announcer read the results of the girls' high jump. Elizabeth had placed second. The hurdlers passed. Elizabeth crossed the track. She walked up into the stands. "I lost on scratches," said. She shrugged. "Five feet." It was five inches below her best.

The state track meet continued the next day, Saturday, and I was there. We all were. Susan was a volunteer on the field. Dad was helping again, too. This left me and Mom in the stands, in the sun. Elizabeth wasn't competing in any other events, so today she wasn't even in her track uniform. She sat with Wayne.

Elizabeth enjoyed watching Wayne run. He ran so smoothly. He wasn't a natural talent, but he had the ability to ignore pain. His 3,200-meter relay team won fourth place, which was good. The team was Wayne, Erik Salmons, Stan Henson, and Greg Starr. Greg was a freshman, believe it or not, and later when he won the 3,200-meter run, everyone was just sort of amazed.

Elizabeth arranged it so she could ride home with Wayne and their friend Jay. Prom was tonight, and they had a couple of errands to run. She and Wayne and Jay walked into the parking lot at the end of the afternoon. Next to Jay's car was a souped-up classic Mustang.

"Pretty nice ride, eh?" Jay said, nodding at the Mustang.

Elizabeth looked at it. It did look good. Glossy orange paint. Jacked up in the back. It must have had some body work done or something, though, because the windows didn't meet the roof in a straight line.

"Yeah, but look at the windows," Elizabeth said.

"Could fix that," Wayne said. "Or you could just drive around with the windows open." He bent and peeked in the windows. Elizabeth looked in, too. She could see cassette tapes in the backseat. Dave Edmonds.

"Well, they like Dave Edmonds, just like you," she said.

"Good taste," Wayne said. "I say we take this car."

"Oh, yeah, let's just steal it," Elizabeth scoffed.

Then Wayne reached into the pocket of his sweatpants and pulled out a key and put the key in the door of the Mustang and opened the door and got in and Elizabeth just sort of watched him do all of this, and as her amazement escalated she found herself dumbstruck and finally all she said was "Wayne!"

He'd been dropping hints about some surprise for prom, and so this was it. He'd bought a cool car. Or—well—he was "test-driving" the car for the weekend, having convinced the owner that he was seriously considering buying it. They drove out of the parking lot, waving to Jay, who had been in on the whole plan, and Elizabeth said the car sounded like an airplane, which was to say that it was loud, but Wayne said that it was a good kind of loud, and just then they turned out of the parking lot, and Wayne floored it and it took off.

They went and picked up her nosegay.

Elizabeth got home at 4:10 a.m. after prom. She'd had no curfew that night. She slept until noon. Then she worked on her final paper for Mrs. Engelbrecht. After an early dinner, she and Dad went to Jeff City to the capitol. They walked through the concrete-block tunnel that connected the parking garage to the capitol basement. Dad unlocked the glass door that led into his office, and he turned on the fluores-cent lights and they buzzed. She worked on the computer, compos-ing and recomposing, and finally typed out her paper on the nice typewriter so it was just right. Dad proofread, helped her with the computer, gave little suggestions here and there, bought them each a snack from the vending machines, but mainly sat by and read. At about 1:00 a.m., they finished and went home. Her paper was about Coleridge, and Mrs. Engelbrecht collected the papers the next day in class. Mrs. Engelbrecht was the best teacher in the school. Today she was terse. She stood behind her desk, straightening the pile of papers. She said, "I honestly look forward to reading these papers. I know it may sound strange, but I enjoy seeing the extent to which your writing has improved over the course of the year. It gives me great satisfaction. If I've been ill tempered for the past week, I apolo-gize. It's only because after a long year of working with you, and get-ting you all writing at the level you need to be writing at, now you're all about to leave, and I'll have to start all over with the next class in the fall." She put the papers into a folder. "But I will enjoy reading these," she said. "I truly will."

Wayne came over that night and he and I went down to the pond. He had some strange ideas about fishing. He was intent on hooking a huge catfish. I wasn't sure there were any catfish in the pond anymore, and I selected a lure based on my experience and the conditions and I caught a big bass. Wayne caught nothing. We cleaned the bass, and Mom fried it, and Wayne stayed for dinner. It was the first time Wayne had ever eaten dinner with us. After dinner, Wayne climbed two trees that I considered unclimbable. Then he scaled the silo.

The next week, Elizabeth graduated on Thursday. Her dress was blue. Her robe was white. On Friday, the last day of school, Mom picked up me and Susan. In the back of the station wagon were three big flats of strawberries she'd picked.

A week later, it was June.

You Will Lose More

You will lose more, of course. Elizabeth will be gone in a few months, and that will feel like severing a limb from the body that is your family. Then Susan, too, will leave for college, in just three years, off to another state. Yes, you will get to move into their room, have your own bathroom, your own air conditioner, your own view of the horse pasture and the slope leading down to the pond. No longer will you sleep near the airy openness of the stairwell, hear all the sounds of the first floor; you will have a door that you can shut. That old yellow pine door, glossy with polyurethane. When your sisters lived here, if the lights were on in their room, and the lights were off in your room, there was a thin place in one of the door's panels where the light would shine through, making a red, glowing stain. You would see it as you fell asleep. It meant your sisters were in there. Your sisters were awake. Now you are behind that door, and there's no one on the other side.

You will use the same blue desk that Elizabeth used—the one with the white drawer knobs—tucked away in the little alcove between the closet and the bathroom door. You'll have a computer then, and even your own little black-and-white television, and in high school you will spend a thousand nights there. But loneliness is not your enemy; it is a companion of sorts. And besides, there will be a girl, finally, and she will call you, and you will call her, and you will write eighty-six letters to her in 1990, and she will write eighty-three back. An upside-down stamp signifies love. She will live sixteen miles away. She will flop down onto your bed at three a.m. after your senior prom. You two will have ridden the four-wheeler across the front hill and nearly run into a skunk. You will have lain side by side in sleeping bags looking at the stars. Pretty soon after that night, you will leave for college, too, and leave her behind, and drive east with Dad in a car loaded with your possessions, and a hollowness in your gut that was carved out when you said goodbye to her, and when you get to college and get the key to your mailbox—just a couple days after leaving home—you will unlock your mailbox, and there will already be a letter there. From her. Sleep tight, my love.

Elizabeth will leave. Susan will leave. You will leave.

When you were small—very small—you thought that one day you had to choose one of your sisters to marry. When you were small, very small, you called Elizabeth "Bess" and Susan "Girl." When you were small, very small, you had a green rubber ball that pleased you completely. It bounded across the lawn.

A few weeks after you received Teddy for your birthday, your mother brought him to your kindergarten room, and your class sat in a circle on the floor, and Teddy the puppy ran around inside the circle.

You have spent hours and hours of your life playing in the gravel driveway in the rain. You diverted the rivulets, dammed them, floated twigs in them. Water flowing, water going, water staying.

On the day you turn thirteen, Susan will blow bubbles, and you will chase the bubbles with a stick across the pasture, swinging at them, and this hour will be one of the happiest of your life.

Grandpa will die, too, of course, during the summer when you are twenty-three, and you will drive down from Iowa into western Missouri, pick up your sisters at the Kansas City airport, and then you will all three go to Windsor for the funeral. The summer he dies will be remarkably cool, and crickets will sing throughout the summer, as if it were just one extended September.

He will have the same disease she had.

The family will sell Grandma and Grandpa's farm, the land that has been in the family for over a century, and you will wonder to

yourself if now, for the first time in your life, it is time to step forward
and speak up. Maybe an arrangement could be made whereby you
live on the farm, and farm it, and keep it in the family, and pay off
your father and Kent in time. You will recognize the value of rightness. You will appreciate the importance of place. You will picture
yourself wearing a straw cowboy hat and driving a red tractor. So,
you will consider all that, but you will not do it, not even say anything. A month after the funeral, you and the family will come back
to the farm for the auction. Your family, and Kent and Lucretia's family. The last time you will be here together. You will go through the
kitchen cabinets and discover appliances and dishes that have not
been moved since Grandma died. Your mother will find some of her
clothes at the bottom of the laundry hamper.

You will eventually give Toni Renken the little red heart earrings. It
will be in eighth grade, and the occasion will be her birthday, and
she will thank you, but that will be the end of it. You will never see
her wear the earrings, and you will wonder about them for the rest
of your life, those earrings that lived in a box under your bed for
three years.

You will continue to like Toni, though, and you will someday
look back and realize that you pined for her from second grade
through the end of your sophomore year—at which point you met
the girl to whom you wrote eighty-six letters in 1990. Really, though,
you will still like Toni, even when you have a girlfriend, and so actually you will have liked her from the day you noticed her running
past you on the playground in second grade until the very last time
you saw her, which was the morning after your high school graduation. After that, it will become more difficult to like her, because you
will live far away and never see or talk with her, and she will marry
rather early, and you will remember less and less of her, and you
never had a chance with her anyway.

There will be a night on your senior trip when your whole
high school class is on a cruise on a lake near Branson, when Toni

will persuade you to undo your ponytail and let her run her fingers through your hair for half an hour while you both sit at the prow of the boat as it pushes through the night.

Christmas will be changed. Christmas will be remembered as the time when Grandma was sick, even though that will almost never be mentioned. There will never be a Christmas like there was when Grandma was alive. You will be getting too old anyway, but regardless, through your teenage years Christmas will continue to carry the burden of the memories of the year she got sick, and even into your twenties, and your thirties, and you will wonder if Christmas will ever be free of that weight. The burden that Christmas brings is not a simple burden, but a knot of not-feeling and pain, and there will be a part of you that is still eleven years old, and will always be eleven years old. And all this will be reinforced when you are in high school and your great aunt Billie is walking home from delivering Christmas cookies to a nursing home a week before Christmas, when she is crossing the street at the crosswalk and is hit by a truck. She will be in a coma through Christmas and into the new year, and then she will die, and you will not go to the funeral—you will never quite understand why your parents didn't make you—and you will spend the night of her funeral sitting at your desk with your computer games and your sitcoms.

And the first time you come home from college, Christmas 1991, you will discover that you have asthma. Apparently, you were allergic to your house and the cats and the farm the whole time you were growing up, but your body had grown accustomed to it, but now that you have left and come back the allergies will rise up and constrict the tiny passageways in your lungs, and you will wake up every night of Christmas vacation at three or four a.m. struggling to get your breath, and you will sit up in the kitchen long past midnight on New Year's Eve, trying to breathe, having already taken more of your medication than you are supposed to, and you will just sit there, working to breathe, realizing that your connection to the living world is tenuous. But you will make it.

You had loved the cats, but now they will be your enemies. Tracks, that little black cat: your enemy.

That Christmas, too, will see your reunion with the girl to whom you wrote eighty-six letters in 1990, four months after you had to leave for college, and you will be full of hopes and expectations and ready for the coming together and the renewed sense of rightness and completeness that you expect to occur, but though the reunion is nice, it is made clear to you that the girl to whom you wrote eighty-six letters in 1990 has let go of the boy to whom she wrote eighty-three letters in 1990. It took her less than four months to let go of you, but it will take you a long time before you let go of her. But you will.

Who are you? You will still be finding out. You will come into your senior year of college, and you will be getting closer to being the self you wanted yourself to be, but in December, late one night in your room, you will suddenly see flashes and strobes of light, growing larger like mutant ice crystals, and you will think you are dying and going blind and going crazy and your body will shake and you will go look at yourself in the bathroom mirror and even though the lights in your eyes fade after twenty minutes you will make an appointment to see an ophthalmologist and he will be a kind and seasoned doctor, and he will examine you, and then he will take out a pad of paper and draw some squiggly lines for you and ask you if that is what the lights in your eyes looked like, and you will say yes, that is exactly what they looked like, and he will tell you what they are—they are harmless—and you will be relieved for about a day, but then you will start to notice more blips and flashes in your eyesight, or at least think you see more blips and flashes in your eyesight, and you will call the ophthalmologist and beg for another appointment and you will get one, and this time he will give you a full exam, and he will reassure you that you are completely fine—there is nothing wrong.

You will be on a path, though, going down a path to someplace bad. And you will be home for Christmas a couple of weeks later, battling through the nights with that cruel demon, asthma—the demon who lives only in the house where you grew up—and when you take your medicine at two a.m. one morning, something will happen: your heart will race and start to skip beats, and you will feel like your blood is suddenly electrified, searing all your blood vessels, and your hands will shake uncontrollably, and your mind will feel miswired—or unwired, as if its vital connections have broken loose—and you will try to calm down, try to relax, but it will not work, it will not work at all, and you will draw a bath to help you relax, but it will not work, it will not work at all, and over the next several days you will get little sleep, and you will have more of these panic attacks, and when you're not having panic attacks you will feel anxious and depressed, worrying about when the next wave of panic will come, and where it will come from, and why, and you will still have these episodes when you return to college—the campus buried under snow, the northern sun dropping far too early into the trees every day—and you will visit a psychologist on campus and he will get you to talk, and he will say, have you ever been depressed before? And you will say, I don't really think I'm depressed now. And he will say that depression and anxiety are two weeds that grow in the same garden. And he will get you to remember that you had some troubles with anxiety long ago, when you were ten. It had been the winter of fourth grade, you will tell him, and you and your fellow Cub Scouts were playing basketball after school, when suddenly you couldn't catch your breath. You were hyperventilating, but it felt like you were dying, and the fear that moved into you then was huge. You started having trouble sleeping. You worried. You worried about sleeping (and no amount of concentration would help you sleep). You worried about breathing. You wondered if you were doing it right. You would lie awake and worry, and your chest would start to hurt. How often were you supposed to breathe? Were you doing it right? If you were doing it right, how come it hurt? Then, still talking with the psychologist, you will remember that Elizabeth had been caught in a storm that spring; she'd been coming home and a storm had thrown a bunch of gravel at her truck and she'd jumped out of the truck and run to the ditch, and after that you were scared of storms—terrified of them—and they made you cold and made you shake. And soon, too, you started worrying about swallowing. You worried that your food was getting stuck in your throat—you could feel it in there, accumulating—and this made it difficult to eat because eating made you worry, eating made you feel that lump of food in your throat, which you were certain would block your windpipe at any moment. So these things all came together—worrying about breathing, worrying about swallowing, worrying about storms—and they stuck with you for weeks, for months. They did gradually subside, but their footprints remained in you—you could feel them there— and now here you were, twenty-one years old—old enough not to worry about breathing and swallowing and storms—but again fear had taken root inside you, and smudged out the fun of living and sapped your core. Of course that was also the year, you will tell the psychologist, that your grandmother died, the grandmother you all loved so much—she was like a grandmother out of a storybook— and also that your sister went far away to college. So. So it was a hard year for a boy. Fear and loss. Loss and fear. Talk about two weeds that grow in the same garden.

Did you start to feel anxious before or after your grandmother died? he will ask.

I don't know, you'll say. Both? Neither? It will not be an answer that satisfies him.

It's something to think about, he will say.

What does that mean? you will wonder. Isn't *everything* something to think about?

And many years after talking to that psychologist, you will gloss over some of this while recording your memories in a book. You will depict that summer after fourth grade as golden and rich, whereas really you had been afraid to eat bread because of the lump it made in your throat, and you had been afraid of dark clouds because of their potential for destruction. You will make it look as if things started to go bad when Grandma got sick, but things had started to go bad earlier that year, on a warm day in February when you hyperventilated, so actually your book will not be entirely accurate on that account.

Still, you will tell yourself, your book depicts a version the truth—one of many—and after all it is a stylized account of events that happened so long ago that to record them with any degree of accuracy is still an exercise in creativity. Let the golden summer stand. Let it speak for the Before. Let the rest speak for the After.

When you were ten, you remember, your mother's remedy for your anxiety was to take you on long bike trips through the summer countryside. You didn't think too much about the reason behind the bicycle tours at the time—Mom was always coming up with novel activities. You just went happily along because it was a grand adventure, after all, and you had recently acquired a black Schwinn three-speed bicycle that was gorgeous and fast. Mom rode a clunky old ten-speed that had been her father's. You would sit together at the kitchen table after breakfast and look at the topographical map of the countryside and think about what roads you could explore. You would strike out midmorning with a backpack containing water and a little bag of sunflower seeds and raisins. You would roll down the hills into the North Moreau Creek bottomlands, cross one of the low water bridges—which meant getting your feet wet—then pedal boldly into the strange and wonderful territory that was only a few miles from your house, but which you'd never seen.

There were crowds of hills, one after another, and a big dairy farm that sat right by the road, and several dogs that gave chase. Over one rambling creek there was a wooden bridge of advanced age, the visual impression of which communicated great precariousness. Some of the gravel roads you explored were so small that they were just two tracks where wheels kept the crabgrass from growing. And such strange road names: Dynamite Ridge, Wieneke Branch, Rockhouse. It had the feel of a foreign country that just happened to look amazingly like your homeland, like how sometimes at home you would hold up a mirror and observe the landscape behind you and wonder at how beautifully strange and yet completely known it looked.

You acquired, on those rides, a fondness for the raucously weedy ditches of Missouri. You drank water. You downshifted. You pedaled hard uphill. Mom and you. What a good mother. What adventure. The cool shade of West Meller Road led to the road's harrowing descent down the bluff above the creek. There in the calm pool above the ford, you could skip stones all day. A snapping turtle sunned itself on a log. Pedaling along. When cars passed you, they engulfed you in great clouds of dust, but you didn't mind.

The landscape was hills and small pastures, but the language of the landscape was shadow and light. Hot, bright expanses of mown hay fields. Dark cedar thickets growing right up to an abandoned barn. Rich bottomland fields with dense stands of corn. Cows grazing their way uphill, inserting their snouts into the shadows of the tall grass. Patches of shade thrown onto the bright gravel road by the pin oaks and red oaks. Six miles, eight miles, nine miles. Your accomplishments could be measured. You would arrive home, ready for lunch—dusty, exhausted, full of summer.

Do you think those bike rides helped you? the psychologist in college will ask.

I don't know. I guess. But if they did help me forget my anxiety, or at least control it, I suppose that my grandmother's illness and death soon thereafter, and my sister's flight to a college far, far away, was a double dose of loss that acted as a kind of catalyst to turn that anxiety into something permanent, deep, and dark.

He will nod.

Just tell me what's wrong and what's right! you will want to say.

How can anxiety and numbness coexist in one person? you will wonder. How does that make sense at all?

You will talk with that psychologist several times, and though he will help you realize that anxiety has been within you since you were ten years old, the overall therapeutic effect of your talks with him will be nil—in fact you will think perhaps you are worse after talking to him because, after all, there is nothing more depressing than talking about depression—and you will still be having panic attacks that make you walk out of seminars in the middle of class, and worrying that you are going blind, and sleeping little, and making drawings in your art class so dark and gorgeous that the instructor will pause in front of them—an instructor who has seen it all—and say, "Wowzers," and step close to look at the details, then step away to take in the overall impression, and say, "That is intense and abrupt." And a few days after your twenty-second birthday, your parents will call to report that your dog, Teddy, has died. Also, your grandfather will begin his final illness about this time.

Finally, the psychologist will refer you to a psychiatrist, and the psychiatrist will write a prescription, and the pills will be a milky-pink and five-sided like the home plate on a baseball diamond, and the pills will work.

In high school, you will lifeguard in Russellville, just like your sisters did. You will drive the same truck Susan and Elizabeth did. You will fishtail.

You'll never be much of a high jumper, by the way. You will do fine the summer after fifth grade in the Junior Olympics, and pretty good in sixth grade, but more and more you will worry about landing on the bar and breaking your back, and more and more you will encounter substantial competition, and by the time you are in eighth grade you will hate the high jump and realize you were probably only good at it when you were younger because there were hardly any other kids doing it.

Gosh, golly, and gee whiz.

Right now, though, you're still eleven years old. It's May. Your grandmother has died, but your sister has not left for college yet.

Under the Summer Sun

That summer we had the high jump pit at home. Mom and Dad asked the school if we could borrow it, so Elizabeth could keep jumping after track season was over. The school agreed, and at the beginning of June, Dad and I drove to the school in the pickup. The head custodian and Dad dragged the high jump pit—that bag of foam blocks—from the back of the maintenance shed and loaded it into the bed of the pickup. We also took the two uprights that held the bar, and the bar itself.

At home, we stored the pit in the part of the barn that connected the silo to the barn. In the evening, two or three times a week, Elizabeth and I would drag it out and set it up in the barnyard. Its sudden appearance always scared the cats. Elizabeth and I would take turns jumping. At first, it was novel and exciting that we had the high jump pit at home, but soon enough it became just another part of the summerscape: the gritty concrete deck at the swimming pool, thunderstorms on the horizon, firecrackers dropped into tin cans, dust blown off the softball diamond, the high jump pit smelling like the barn.

That big bag of foam.

I got a new bike. It had registered with me that my still-newish black three-speed—with its silver fenders and curving top tube and mustache handlebars—was not entirely cool, especially when compared with a new BMX bike. BMX stood for "bicycle motocross," and the bikes were small and agile, with knobby tires. They were designed for racing on dirt tracks, and they were good at jumping—as I had seen in a magazine—and a certain new kid in Susan's class, one Tracy Price, who had come from someplace many degrees cooler than Russellville, rode a BMX bike, and he assured me it was the only kind of bike worth riding—and judging from the attention he got from girls, he was right. If I owned such a bike, it would be an external representation of my internal coolness.

The bike I wanted was much better than the Huffys my friends had. It was called "Predator," and it had a sleek silver frame made with a steel alloy that was lighter than normal steel, and the price was $250.00 plus tax. It was a jaw-dropping price, the kind of price that at first didn't even make sense. (Was the price tag wrong? Was the bike made of gold?) I had never owned anything worth that much. In fact, the list of things my family owned that cost more than the bike was pretty short: the farm, the house, the vehicles, the trailer, our big freezer, Dad's camera, the television, and the livestock. But the price of the bike, of course, confirmed that it was a thing worth having.

Eventually, after enough campaigning, Mom and Dad agreed that I could get the Predator. Then began the difficult negotiations about the way in which I would go about paying for such a thing. It eventually came down to this: trade-in of old bike $70.00; savings, $64.21; cutting cedar trees, $12.76; June allowance, $8.00; and the balance of $107.80 to be deducted from my allowance in ten installments over ten months. For a total of $262.77.

Then I had it. I had the bike. June 11, 1984, it was mine. I took it with me to one of Susan's softball games, where it was widely admired, and I bragged about exactly how little it weighed and how fast it went. I let its appearance speak for its abilities, though, and I didn't accept any challenges to race. Not right now, I said. Besides, it was designed for dirt racing, not street racing.

Tracy Price was impressed with the bike, and he explained to me that to take care of it I should clean it regularly and store it inside.

Elizabeth worked two jobs to save money for college. Dad helped her get a job with the state. She worked on the eighth floor of the new Truman Building, and though the job sounded good and paid okay, she quickly tired of it. It felt like prison. File, file, file. (Paper cuts!) Stamp this, stamp that, open mail, don't wear jeans. *Tick, tick, tick*—the second hand on the clock moved too slowly. She worked in offices where there were no windows, and at the end of the day she would ride the long escalators down through the building's huge, open atrium, and walk out the doors and into the heat of the afternoon and to her it felt like waking up.

At night she would lifeguard from six until nine, and she liked the way the summer sun eased slowly toward the horizon, then how the underwater lights came on in the pool, and the moths came to the big floodlights overhead, and Wayne would wait outside the chain-link fence for her shift to be over.

And though she was asked to lifeguard on the Fourth of July, she said that she couldn't, and instead Wayne picked her up in his blue tank of a car (the orange Mustang just a memory) and they drove to Jeff City together, rolling down Missouri Boulevard—once, twice, then back a third time, toward downtown—and with the windows all down—all four of them—and the tinny stereo tuned to the only decent rock station, Wayne put his arm around Elizabeth—who was sitting in the middle of the bench seat—and he accelerated and said, "Eliza*best*, Betsy, my baby!" and it sounded so good. They parked not far from where she worked, and they walked up toward the capitol, and the sidewalks were crowded, and the streets busy, and at almost ten o'clock the fireworks started, and boomed and flashed over the capitol dome and over the Missouri River, and as the show continued, the fireworks slowly moved away—the fireworks barge was drifting downstream—and she felt good, and everything seemed okay for a little while. She was with Wayne.

I discovered the sport of horsefly hunting. Under the summer sun, the west pond had shrunk, exposing a few feet of mud around its perimeter. I would take my BB gun down there and crouch on the shore, waiting for the big droning horseflies to come—you could hear them as they approached—and land on the mud to drink. Then they were mine, assuming they were within about ten feet of me. I would steady my BB rifle on my knee and line up the horsefly carefully in the sights, inhale, hold my breath, then gently squeeze the trigger. It was a sniper job.

But in the middle of my fifth afternoon sniping horseflies, I suddenly just quit. I had a big horsefly in my sights and my finger on the trigger, but instead of firing I lowered my rifle and watched the horsefly. He just wanted a drink of water, after all. After a while he flew away. I sat there, disappointed in myself for killing flies for no reason, and then I aimed my gun at the pond and fired the BB into the water. I didn't hunt horseflies anymore after that.

A Day Made for Grape Juice

I had a party that summer. I realized that if I hosted a party I would be in control of the guest list and also, as the host, I would be the most important person there. Mom said it would be fine if I had a party. And I had not seen Toni since the end of school, and this was an aggravation. I had often daydreamed of her that summer, like when I was cutting cedar trees in the pastures and imagined her seeing me doing this work—being impressed, and maybe later offering me some lemonade.

This was the guest list: Brad, Toni, Jeena. This guest list made sense: the two main characters and their foils.

On the appointed day, we all met in the parking lot in front of the school, which was an empty and foreign-seeming place in the summertime. Then we had some good conversation during the drive to my house. Mom was pretty good at coming up with good topics—had anyone taken any trips this summer, and what did we want on our pizza, and so forth. At home, we four went up to my room. Toni had never been to my house before, and now here she was in my very room, looking at my things, seeing my pillow, walking on my carpet, and observing the view from my windows.

We all settled down on the carpet and watched a video tape of an animated movie about some rodents. Brad, Toni, and Jeena had not seen it before. I had, and it was one of my favorite movies. The TV—a big nineteen-incher that Mom and Dad had bought in April after living forever with only a tiny black-and-white TV—had been moved to my room, and just a few weeks ago they had bought a video cassette recorder, too. The whole idea of watching a movie at home—whichever one I wanted, whenever I wanted—was so fantastic that it was like living in a dream world where anything was possible.

We watched the movie. It contained friendly rodents, bad rodents, an evil cat, and a goofy crow named Jeremy. Indeed! We munched popcorn and drank juice. And though the real me loved the movie, there was a part of me that felt self-conscious about watching it with friends, because it wasn't the coolest movie in the world. It was a kids' movie.

Lunch was homemade pizza, which the four of us helped to top. Mom made the best pizza—crust and all—and we had a good time eating and drinking yet more juice.

It was a day made for grape juice.

After lunch, there was some business where Toni and Jeena were still downstairs while Brad and I were upstairs, and Brad told me something Jeena had said that Toni had said, and then he said that maybe I could tell him a response that he could pass on to Jeena, who would tell it to Toni. I could hear the girls whispering downstairs, and I crept to the edge of the stairwell and overheard something about somebody maybe liking somebody else blah blah blah boyfriend. Then Toni and Jeena were suddenly coming up the stairs, and Brad and I had to scramble away so it didn't look like we'd been listening. They came up the stairs, not talking, and we were there in the middle of the floor, not talking, and there was a whole lot of not-talking going on.

Later, I proposed an excursion. There was a bluff at the back of the farm that had a good view of the river valley. I thought it was an interesting and mature sort of thing to engineer an outing. I liked the idea of Toni seeing me outside, on the farm, walking across the landscape, showing her the wonderful view.

It was hot outside—typical August broiler weather—but we decided we could handle it. We walked back past the barn, down through the barn pasture, and into the north pasture. We followed the fenceline north. We could see the bluff to which we were headed.

But as we prepared to climb the fence, we noticed that something was on us. Something was crawling on us—all four of us. We looked close. Real close. And we saw that our ankles and lower legs were covered with baby ticks, swarms of them. They were the smallest of all baby ticks, so small that they looked like scattered pepper. The only way we could tell they were ticks was that they were moving. Moving up.

We all headed back to the house, and Mom helped the girls wash their legs in the bathtub while Brad and I washed our legs in a bucket of soapy water outside, and Mom threw everyone's socks in the washing machine. The party moved to the front porch, and we all sat out there, barefoot, on the porch swing. Soon Toni's mom called and said she was coming to get Toni slightly early. Within half an hour they were all gone.

They did get to take their socks home, even though they were still wet.

But any way I looked at it, there was no way in which the party could be judged anything more than a marginal success. Animated mice, grape juice, swarms of baby ticks, wet socks . . . It was not what I had envisioned.

Meanwhile, my glorious new bike had also failed to live up to the expectations I had heaped on it. I continued, as the summer waned, to be extremely enthusiastic about not riding that bike much. Sometimes I would ride it around the yard, pretending to be racing, then lean it up against a tree and admire it. I did build a small jump in the barnyard by piling up some dirt, but no matter how fast I rode toward this jump, the bike didn't ever get airborne. It just went up one side of the dirt mound and down the other.

I was starting to realize BMX might not be my sport. The nearest BMX racetrack, for example, was an hour and a half away. Still, I kept the bike inside. I cleaned it with soft rags, though not as often as I had at first.

It wasn't even a particularly fast bike. The three-speed had been faster, even though it was heavier and completely uncool. But the three-speed had a speedometer. The three-speed had carried me far and wide over the countryside. The three-speed had *three speeds.* But the three-speed was gone, and though I had the coolest bike in the school district, it had not changed my life. I liked my old bike.

What did it mean that a $250.00 bike was not all that fast? What did it mean that the coolest bike in the world was not as good as my dorky old bike? I didn't understand. What was wrong with the world?

East

On the morning of August 21, 1984, after three a.m., Elizabeth drove home. She cruised through the dark neighborhoods of Russellville, and just before she left town, she stopped and rolled down the windows. Then she accelerated onto the road home, and the humid late summer air filled the truck cab, swirling around her, and all she could hear was the wind and the truck's engine. When she got home, the house was dark. She parked the pickup, walked up the sidewalk, came in the back door—it wasn't locked—and put the truck keys in the little tray beside the door. She had carried this set of keys for two years, but now she wouldn't need them.

She didn't turn on any lights. No one was waiting up for her. She hadn't had a curfew. She made her way through the dark kitchen, the darker living room, and up the stairs. The stairwell railing guided her through my room and into her and Susan's room. She turned on her little desk lamp. She draped a T-shirt over the lamp to dim it. She saw Susan there on the trundle bed, asleep on her stomach.

Elizabeth took out her contacts. She brushed her teeth. Then she sat at her desk and got out her journal. She wrote about tonight, about saying goodbye to Wayne. Then at the end of the page she wrote, *Final entry*. She closed the journal and put it in the bottom drawer of her desk.

She got into bed and closed her eyes, and for a short time she was asleep, but it wasn't long before she became aware of dawn filling the window. When she finally sat up, giving up on sleep, it was 5:20. She got dressed.

The rest of us were up early, too, though not unreasonably early. We had worked all of yesterday getting ready, and much of the packing and preparations were done. In fact, Elizabeth was completely done with packing, and her bags and boxes were piled in the living room waiting for Dad to carry them to the car. She'd finished all her work before going out with Wayne last night.

This wasn't to say we didn't have more work to do. We did. Mom had the cooler of food to prepare. On car trips we always took a huge cooler of food, so we could save money and eat healthy. Meanwhile, Dad had the task of packing the car. This was one of his special skills, yes, but we were not packing simply for a weeklong trip, but for a weeklong trip that included taking Elizabeth to Cornell, along with all her stuff. Our station wagon was not equal to this amount of cargo, so for this trip we used a car-top carrier. Still, space was tight, and Dad's job was complex.

As for me, I spent time choosing books and games to bring, then I just carried out any request that Mom or Dad saw fit to throw at me. Susan was in essentially the same position as I was, although she was also scrambling to finish up packing.

So the four of us were busy. But Elizabeth—the whole reason for this trip, and therefore the whole reason for the bustle—was calm and quiet. Her packing done, her breakfast eaten, she wandered upstairs, then back downstairs, not saying much, not really interacting with the rest of us. She wandered out the back door.

I saw her outside when I was refreshing the pan of drinking water for Teddy. She was in the barnyard, standing by the horses, rubbing their muzzles. The sun was up, bright and warm, and the farm was lit up beautifully.

We did our last-minute chores—washing the dishes, tidying the house, vacuuming—and then we were ready to go. The checklist was complete. Car packed. Food packed. Animals fed. Humans fed. House clean. Windows closed. Gas tank full. Dad ready. Mom ready. Susan ready. Me ready. And we knew Elizabeth was ready.

But Elizabeth was scarce. In fact, she was so scarce, she did not seem to be present. Where was Elizabeth? We called for her. We searched the house. No Elizabeth. When was the last time any of us had seen her? I reported having seen her with the horses about an hour ago. No one seemed to have seen her after that.

We checked the horses. They were both still here. At least she hadn't saddled one of them and absconded over the hills.

We split up. Dad searched the barn and the north pastures. Susan checked the house again and walked up the driveway. Mom looked in the cellar house, in the chicken house, and around the garden. We called for her as we went.

I looked down the hill at the pond. Then I had the brainstorm that maybe she was in the pickup. Maybe she was asleep in there.

She was not.

While I was looking under my bed, the phone rang. Who would be calling us? I heard the back door close and footsteps approach the phone in the kitchen. Mom answered the phone.

"Where are you?!" I heard her say. Then she said, "Russellville? How'd you get to Russellville?"

She ran.

Well, all her stuff was already packed, ready to go. So we locked the house, I said goodbye to Teddy, and we drove the six miles to Russellville. We pulled up in front of Wayne's house and Elizabeth came out and got in the car and we waved to Wayne's mother and then we left. We headed east.

Elizabeth told us that she hadn't planned it. She'd just been out walking around the farm, sort of saying goodbye to it. She had started walking up the driveway. Then she reached Mount Hope Road and kept walking. Then she started running, and then she kept running, and she went to Wayne.

But when she reached Wayne's house, he wasn't there. His mother said he'd arisen early and gone for a long run.

After the start, our trip was not remarkable. We weren't traveling for pleasure. Our mission was one of separation. So this changed the timbre of the hours, and the interstate miles rolled along dully, and no one can make a case for the midwestern stretches of Interstate 70 being scenic. We stayed the first night in Indiana, then passed into Ohio in the morning.

This mission of separation. I didn't want Elizabeth to be elsewhere. I wanted her at home, or on the farm, or in Russellville, or doing fishtails in the pickup truck, or at a track meet somewhere, high jumping like nobody's business. To put Elizabeth outside of these places was to upset the balance of what was good, and it had already been upset once this year. Then, to see Elizabeth run to Wayne's house, to see her own dread of separation, only made it harder to endure.

On the second day, we went through heavy rain, darkness, and sad industrial towns. The next morning, though, was fair, and we pushed on into New York, and the land became gorgeous and green and it was like a landscape from out of a poem—glaciated hills, dense woods, lush pastures. We reached Ithaca around noon and checked into a hotel. We discovered that the rain last night had soaked everything in the car-top carrier—most of which was Elizabeth's stuff. Mom laid the wet clothes out in the hotel room to dry. After lunch, Mom and the girls took the car for some errands. Dad and I walked to a bicycle shop and rented two bikes, then rode the back streets through town, up the hill, and around campus. Long ago, Dad had had a postdoctorate fellowship here, and he was happy seeing the campus again. It was a beautiful day, and a beautiful campus, and the first time I saw the view from the library out across the lake and on into the hills, I felt in awe. So this, too, exists.

It seemed a place worthy of Elizabeth.

That evening we picnicked on the shore of Cayuga Lake—the long, glacial lake I'd seen from campus—and the sunlight was clear and low, and we ate, and fed bread to the ducks—mommies and babies—and seagulls—seagulls!—and the wind was pushing wavelets against the shore, and out there, on the blue water, were sailboats—real sailboats!—and Susan and Elizabeth and I rode on a carousel, and then we went back to the edge of the water and watched the sun go lower. We had the little park to ourselves.

In the morning, we packed the car with Elizabeth's stuff and drove up to campus. Approaching Elizabeth's dorm, we encountered the cars of other freshmen's families. Mom, Susan, and Elizabeth got out and went to check in. Dad and I were directed to a loading dock at the back of the dorm. We pulled up there, and several students in red Cornell T-shirts whisked all of Elizabeth's stuff into the dormitory.

We went up to her room, and Mom and Elizabeth and Susan were there, and Mom thought the room was shabby with its banged-up furniture, curtains with loose hems, and windows that looked as though they'd leak lots of cold air come winter. She then promptly started re-hemming the curtains with her emergency needle and thread.

We met Elizabeth's roommate, who was an Italian girl from Long Island, and approximately a foot shorter than Elizabeth, and we took a picture of them together outside, and then it was time for us to go. We said goodbye without tears or many words, and we walked away, and turned and waved a final time, and a few moments later I looked back and saw Elizabeth moving into the crowd.

We went down to our hotel, packed, checked out, and drove out of town. We kept to the back roads and stopped at two state parks in the afternoon—saw a beautiful waterfall—then made our way onto Highway 17 and sped west. We made it into Pennsylvania, and we stopped at a motel, unloaded, ate cheeseburgers, then drove a few miles up the road to a park on Lake Erie. The beach was covered in flat stones, and Dad and Susan and I skipped rocks on the lake for a long time. The sun was setting, and the lake was becoming calm—smooth, almost—and we had great fun. Susan and I walked out a long concrete jetty that was just an inch or two above the water. It gave us the feeling of walking on water. We went out quite far. The whole sky was lit up. Then we realized our feet were wet and that water was starting to come over the jetty. The water was rising? Did the Great Lakes have tides?

We walked back to shore. We had two long days of driving in front of us. When we got home, school would start.

As we were about to leave the lakeshore, a bride and groom came down onto the beach. They had appeared from nowhere. The bride had a long white train, and the groom was sharp in his black tuxedo. Behind them came a photographer, and he set up his tripod, and we watched for a little while as he took pictures of the couple on the beach.

Then we left, while there was still light in the sky.

Epilogue

Just one boy. A skinny boy, a boy who was eleven, a boy who could not so much draw dragons as copy them skillfully from picture books, a boy who cried when he killed a sparrow with his BB gun, a boy who mounted stairs two at a time in the same manner as his oldest sister, a boy with a habit of chewing his fingernails, a boy with visions of being a long-distance runner, a boy who liked to laugh, a boy with a troublesome cowlick, a boy with the sky in his heart.

Chickens in the barnyard. The basketball hoop on the side of the barn. Butterflies everywhere. The view from the front hill. Little clouds—a herd of them—moving in unison. The shadow of one. Later, the smell of pie. Close the window. Smoke from the chimney.

Grandma would drive the tractor, and Grandpa would walk behind guiding the walking plow, and they would creep down the length of the garden in one of those low gears that only tractors have, and by the power of the tractor and Grandma's piloting and Grandpa's guiding, the plow blade would slice into the soil and turn it over, revealing dirt that was studded with potatoes.

How many years did they do that together?

And all the thunderstorms and snows and winter winds. All the dark midnights and bright noons and paper sacks full of groceries and half bushels of apples and rows of home-canned green beans on a shelf in the cellar. The drip-drip of water like the tick-tock of the clock, the clock that plays music on the hour, in a world in which music is part of the very fabric of life.

A sewing needle pokes up, pokes down, pulls the thread, makes the seam.

We scatter.

The plow blade turns up more potatoes.

Sitting down to write a letter. To write two letters. To write three letters. The phone doesn't ring. The radio station fades as night comes on.

Home at nite, home at nite, home at nite.

Acknowledgments

First and foremost, my wife, Kelly, deserves copious thanks for helping me get this book written. She was patient and a damn good editor. She came up with the title, too.

My parents and sisters were helpful and understanding and shared with me selflessly their memories and artifacts from the era in question.

For crucial bits of support, guidance, and insight I am grateful to the late Frank Conroy, John Rugge, Kevin Brockmeier, Jennifer Carlson, Daniel Slager, and Allison Wigen.

Support for the writing of this book was provided by the Iowa Arts Council and the National Endowment for the Arts.

The chapter "Food, Animals" appeared in the *Missouri Review* in slightly different form.

I Will Not Leave You Comfortless
Reading Group Guide

1. *I Will Not Leave You Comfortless* has been called "novelistic" even though it is a memoir. Before reading, what were your expectations for a memoir? How has the book met or challenged these expectations?

2. The book is mostly told from the perspective of the author as a fifth-grader, but also includes the perspectives of his sisters, parents, and grandparents. Why do you think Jeremy Jackson chose to do this? What does it add to the story?

3. Which of the three generations of Jacksons (the three siblings, Mom and Dad, or Grandma and Grandpa) did you find most compelling or relatable? Is your answer what you would have expected before reading the book?

4. How did the mixture of generations and time periods in the book make you think about your own notions of history and family? Did it change the way you think about your own family's story?

5. Though many of Jeremy's memories are of family unity, it is also clear that religion was a divisive issue for the Jacksons both between and among generations. Considering this theme, how do you interpret the title of the book—which comes from the bible verse John 14:18? What is the significance of this line to Jackson, despite his spiritual differences from his grandparents?

6. Weather is a recurring theme in the book. The young Jeremy is particularly aware of dangerous weather, and his memories often include the kind of weather that was happening on significant days (like the Christmastime snowstorm). Besides the fact that weather *can* indeed be memorable, why is it significant to Jeremy in the past and the present—as a boy and as an author?

7. What is it like to read the "voice" of a ten-year-old? Do you think Jeremy's young voice would be compelling to younger readers, or does it require an adult maturity to best understand this voice, and why?

8. As consistent as Jeremy's "boy" voice is throughout the book, his mature voice is also undeniably present in some passages, such as when he remembers his Cub Scout Pinewood Derby: "My dreams that spring, my little fantasies, all dissolved into vapor when confronted with the facts and limits of reality" (page 155). What effect did the occasional switch to "adult Jeremy" have on you?

9. Grandma's words are ussed to make up an entire chapter—"Her Existing Sixteen Journal Entries"—and her phrase "home at nite" is repeated as the last line of the book. Why does Jackson include this chapter and return to Grandma's voice at the end? What does his grandmother represent to him?

10. The chapter "You Will Lose More," despite the fact that it reveals much about Jeremy's future, appears a few chapters before the end of the novel, and not as an epilogue as one might expect. Instead, the last few chapters, including the epilogue, return to Jeremy as a ten-year-old. Does this knowledge affect your relationship with Jeremy as the ten-year-old character? What is Jackson saying about memory and identity?

Jeremy Jackson is the author of  the novels *Life at These Speeds* and *In Summer,* as well as three cookbooks, including the James Beard Award nominated *The Cornbread Book.* He has also written novels for teenagers under the name Alex Bradley. He lives near Iowa City, Iowa, and has taught at Vassar College, Grinnell College, and the University of Iowa.

Milkweed Editions

Founded as a nonprofit organization in 1980, Milkweed Editions is an independent publisher. Our mission is to identify, nurture and publish transformative literature, and build an engaged community around it.

Join Us

In addition to revenue generated by the sales of books we publish, Milkweed Editions depends on the generosity of institutions and individuals like you. In an increasingly consolidated and bottom-line-driven publishing world, your support allows us to select and publish books on the basis of their literary quality and transformative potential. Please visit our Web site (www.milkweed.org) or contact us at (800) 520-6455 to learn more.

Milkweed Editions, a nonprofit publisher, gratefully acknowledges sustaining support from Maurice and Sally Blanks; Emilie and Henry Buchwald; the Bush Foundation; the Patrick and Aimee Butler Foundation; Timothy and Tara Clark; Betsy and Edward Cussler; the Dougherty Family Foundation; Mary Lee Dayton; Julie B. DuBois; Joanne and John Gordon; Ellen Grace; William and Jeanne Grandy; John and Andrea Gulla; Elizabeth Driscoll Hlavka and Edwin Hlavka; the Jerome Foundation; the Lerner Foundation; the Lindquist & Vennum Foundation; Sanders and Tasha Marvin; Robert E. and Vivian McDonald; the McKnight Foundation; Mid-Continent Engineering; the Minnesota State Arts Board, through an appropriation by the Minnesota State Legislature and a grant from the National Endowment for the Arts; Christine and John L. Morrison; Kelly Morrison and John Willoughby; the National Endowment for the Arts; Ann and Doug Ness; Jörg and Angie Pierach; the RBC Foundation USA; Deborah Reynolds; Cheryl Ryland; Schele and Philip Smith; the Target Foundation; the Travelers Foundation; Moira Turner; and Edward and Jenny Wahl.

Interior design by Connie Kuhnz
Typeset in Arno Pro
by BookMobile Design & Digital Publisher Services
Printed on acid-free 30% postconsumer-waste paper
by Versa Press, Inc.